The Language Of The Heart:

Is Spoken All Over The World

Tarajyoti Govinda

The Language Of The Heart:
Is Spoken All Over The World
Govinda, Tarajyoti, 1958-1999

First published by Lotus House 1991
Deva Wings Publications 2015

Deva Wings Publications
www.devawings.com
Daylesford, Australia

ISBN 978-0-9587202-1-2

Illustrations by Christine Marchiori
Cover photo by Arjuna Govinda

Deva Wings Publications

Daylesford, Australia
www.devawings.com

To Inner Peace

Chapters

Chapter 1

HIMALAYA

I thought I had everything; tomatoes, onions, potatoes, peas. I had noticed that there were some apples and oranges, fruit I hadn't seen for some time. I filled my knapsack, paid the rupees and began heading towards my home. I could see the mountain path stretch before me and the white water river gushing fast below. The mountain seemed huge, as did the trees. I had been getting fitter. The air and the space were doing me a lot of good. My health seemed to improve and I felt very much alive and excited by the interactions I had had with the Indians. I felt very comfortable just getting a cup of chai.*

I followed the main road until the turn-off and then meandered up the dirt track. It was about a mile and a half up the mountain. I'd come to enjoy this journey. Once a week I went to town for supplies. I had only a modest amount of money and had come to enjoy the bartering at the markets. I had promised a family from another village that I would make chips and they were going to make me an Indian delicacy, a sweet they were sure I would like.

Half way up the track was a seat made of rock that I and many others used as a rest from the journey. I sat down and could see the expanse of the Himalayas before me. I stood on one mountain looking across at the mountain ranges all around me. It was June, summer, and yet they were still snow capped. The altitude was high.

I was content in my Indian garb. I had only two sets of clothes and would wash each day while the other dried. I would spend the mornings in Vashisht* at the sulphur baths which were a part of the temple in the small village. I bathed in the women's section and loved the feel of the warm spring water on my skin. As I sat on the seat overlooking the ranges, I breathed in the air and felt an expanse within me. Everywhere I looked the views were breathtaking. I had come to know intimately, it felt, every aspect of that land, every rock on the path. The mountains exhilarated me. My being was touched in a way that opened me up to the passion of life itself. When I had rested enough, I continued my climb.

I put my vegetables in my house and came back out ready to wash my clothes in the waterfall. I could see Nani across the way. She smiled beamingly at me. I smiled back, feeling my whole energy going in greeting to her. She was sitting in the sun, chopping beans. Nani was typical of some of the women here. She had huge earrings in her ear which made a large hole from the weight. It seemed characteristic of the life itself, the weathered skin reflecting the closeness to nature and the basics of life. The lines on her face made evident the depth of the life experience and they readily formed laughter lines which exuded the energy of joy in the simple things of life. She was always busy preparing food, clothing, keeping things in order and yet always peaceful. There was a sense that she felt one with every moment of life.

I began to wash my clothes on the rocks with my feet. My toes had become quite adept at this and were becoming dexterous at their task.

I loved this lifestyle. I felt so at one with nature here. The man who owned the house I lived in was out in the fields hoeing the land. I was amazed at the work he did in one day, so much strength. I remember within one day he hoed three fields alone.

His wife, Nina, was betrothed to him when she was thirteen and they had five children, all very beautiful. The faces and smiles of the children here touched my heart. The colours of the fabrics they wore added beauty to the land.

I got the potatoes and began to prepare them. Once the clothes were hung out and I could feel the sun on my skin, I could feel Nani's presence even though she was some distance away. We were in a similar state, simply enjoying what is. I had a small Bunsen burner that I used as a stove and a tiny frying pan upon which to cook the chips. I had to cook several frying pans full to get the amount I wanted to share with the family. It was really no bother as I enjoyed it so much. The family arrived and we shared our cultural delicacies with one another. They came from the neighbouring village. I had met them on one of my daily walks. They had invited me in and shared chai. I was thrilled when they responded to my invitation. I felt honoured to be able to return the hospitality.

I had grown so used to eating with my hands and not using knives or forks or spoons. It had become a part of me, my way of life. It was as if life had become like that, with no separation between life and me. No distance. I was finding union in everything, physical and spiritual. We spoke the same language, the language of the heart. The most we could communicate with words was "Hello," "Goodbye," "It's hot," "It's cold." The communication within went a great deal further. In just one glance of eye contact a thousand words were said and we laughed together about simple things.

I said goodbye knowing we'd meet again, perhaps the next day on the track, and went to curl up in my sleeping bag which was placed on a slat of wood. I had no mattress. It did not matter. I felt

3

so good to be close to the hard wood. The floor in my house was made of dirt, I wore no shoes inside. I felt at one with the Earth. I planned the next day to go on a little journey, so before I went to sleep I prepared my knapsack. Full-tummied, filled heart, I slept soundly and woke the next day with the sunshine upon my face and the birds chirping loudly around me.

I set off as usual for my bath in the temple and I followed the track through the pass. The enormity of these mountains struck me everyday. Everyday they were as breathtaking as the first moment I had seen them. I walked for days through these hills and came across towns I didn't know existed, small villages of perhaps ten houses. The houses were rich and lush, made of stone, wood, and hay. The earthy colours contrasted sharply against the blue sky . The light seemed different here from what I was used to in the West. Everything had definition and was full bodied. Even inanimate objects seemed to stand out against their background. There were goats, roosters, bison and children filled with joy running through the streets. They would come to me yelling, "Allo!" often followed by their family. They would smile and meet me through their eyes with their soul. Their hearts spoke. No more need be said. I would sit with these people in these small villages for varying amounts of time, totally unaware of time as such, feeling the meaning in every moment of interaction and feeling the same interaction with the Earth itself, with the valleys, the hills, the tracks, the animals, the birds, the trees.

I was very struck by the sense of family here. I was accepted, it felt, as part of the family everywhere I went. I had been looking for this sense of belonging and found that, in the simplicity of day to day life, one could belong in action, in thought or in deed. One could actually be part of the whole. I could feel the blood flowing through my veins and the fire within, my own heart light radiating from within me, as I encountered everything; people, places and things. It seemed I'd found paradise.

I spent a lot of time when I wasn't walking from village to village, or simply walking along the tracks in the mountains, sitting upon my verandah. Here I wrote letters home to my own family in Melbourne trying to convey the beauty that I had found. I could sense a real communication taking place. When I wasn't writing or doing my daily tasks, I would sit and read or contemplate life, stillness, or I would watch a bird or whatever else came my way as I sat. Months passed and I could feel within much healing taking place. I had liked particularly being with the native Indians within the community. When I would thirst for the companionship of my own culture, people of my culture from Europe, America or Australia would seem to arrive at my doorstep and stay awhile, just enough time for the thirst to be quenched. My every need was met.

One morning I woke, and it was just like every other morning. The birds were chirping. The sun was shining, the land beautiful in aura and Presence. Within me I knew I had to leave. I didn't know why. I just knew I had to. It took some days for this knowing to come fully into my being. It took those days to cherish, for one last moment, all the things I had come to cherish about this place and time within my existence.

The day came when it was time to go. I thought of the contrast of my own being from the day I had arrived until now - such a change. I had been travelling fast for four months through Asia, two or three days was the most I would stop in any one place at any one time. I was searching. My mind raced, my body raced and many other energies within me raced - I needed to stop, to be still, to find peace within, and I had found that, here in the mountains, the Himalayas. I knew as I left that I was taking with me part of those mountains in my heart. They had helped me to awaken to my heart. The mind still, the body full and fit, the heart alive, I left, taking with me an eternal Joy of Being.

The Unexpected Journey

Chapter 2

FINDING GOD IN THE EYES

July 7, 1983 Trincomalee. SRI LANKA

6 p.m. curfew. Martial law. Anyone found on the streets can be shot. Not what I expected. Nonetheless, it was what I found.

I had moved from the beauty and serenity of the Himalayas to come to what I thought would be a tropical paradise, with palm trees and coconuts, sun and sand, pineapples and fish. The eyes of the people were filled with fear, and the body language tense and closed. Everyone went about their business quickly, quietly. No frivolity, no joy.

I was travelling with a girlfriend, Josie. We had met at night class in Melbourne, both of us in stressed western lifestyles and decided we would go travelling together to get away from it all. I had gone earlier to travel some on my own, while she continued working in the hub of the city life. By the time we met up we were in quite different spaces, within and without. I had grown accustomed to life in Asia, my skin and face weathered by the sun, my body thin, fit and agile. I had enjoyed meeting people, being no one in particular, no one's sister, or lover or girlfriend, not a teacher or psychologist, as I had been in Melbourne, not determined by any particular label or role. Many changes had occurred within me over the six months I hadn't seen Josie. It took us some time to adjust to each other. Josie was larger set than I, her hair dark. I loved her wit and enjoyed her company. In spite of our different spaces, it was good to have someone to talk to again, someone who had a similar background.

On arrival at the railway station we were greeted by armoured guards in full uniform. We were hustled into the jeep which took us to our hotel, a tiny guest house, where there were some others like us from France; travellers, a little dismayed by the change in plan. The freedom often found in a traveller's existence was largely curtailed by the looming, civil war. The expected joy and usual high that accompanied the change of country and culture, so often felt in that existence, was not forthcoming. As scene upon scene unfolded of this new journey, more and more restriction, fear and hatred became evident. I could not find the God in their eyes. The usual glow of friendliness, warmth and open heart was nonexistent as the fear and hatred built, an energy that seemed to grow upon itself like a virus, spreading everywhere, even into the core of the earth itself. The crows, which seemed to infiltrate the island, became more and more aggressive as time went by. Swooping and greedy, they scavenged. What sort of a place was I in?

The deathly silence that prevailed after six echoed throughout the whole day in many forms of non-interaction, in the withdrawal of the energies of brotherhood. Even in the children the energy of goodwill left. You could see them, the children, in the day, throwing stones at strangers with hatred in their eyes, throwing stones at each other with little more. This was only an introduction for what was to come.

July 15, 1983. Tirunelveli East

I had heard there was less trouble further north. In the heat of the day, on the stiff seated trucks, we journeyed, in the hope of finding more light. Parched and tired we arrived. Josie went to bed exhausted from the heat and the journey. I craved the cleansing qualities of the sea. My eyes met with a clear eyed, full-bodied Sri

Lankan man who assured me the beach I was looking for was a short distance along the track. I booked into the guesthouse and headed for the sea to find relief for my tired limbs and refreshment for my wearied skin. The countryside itself seemed dry and harsh.

Eventually, after about fifteen minutes I found the sea about which the man was speaking. It was about mid-day and there was not a soul to be seen. I ventured towards the water and peeled off my clothes, leaving my tropical bikinis firmly clenched to my skin. I sat between the water and the sand to take in this moment I had been waiting for. The feeling was divine. An energy entered which caused me to jolt somewhat. Beside me, a little behind me, a naked, strong black man stood, grinning. I felt immediately ill throughout my entire body. He touched me upon the shoulder, a gentle flick and beckoned me to swim with him. I could sense impending danger and shook my head. I stood firmly on the ground and said "No, it is time for me to leave." I began to walk in the direction of my towel which I had thrown on the beach in the excitement of arriving.

A knock in the knee, a punch in the jaw, dragged through the sand into the water, I tried to get my breath, as every few moments my head was forced into the water. I was nearly drowning. His fumbling hands were trying to pull off my bikini. I fought. I had a lot of time, it seemed, to consider this death. It had gone beyond assault, beyond rape, I could see that there was no God in this man's eyes. There was no light that I could appeal to, no rationality, no sanity, just a clear sick abuse of power, a hatred - nothing more. I, the victim of this energy, was feeling as if I could only defend myself and not hurt him. The battle continued for hours, neither one prepared to give up. I was fighting for my life, looking for the God in his eyes, finding none.

I began to find God in the sky, in the sun shining above us. I asked in all earnestness "Why me?" It was then that I knew for the first time consciously that God existed. As I screamed the words, I saw for the first time the choice: to live or to die, to believe or to doubt. I decided to choose life.

The man stopped and I arose, leaving behind a past existence. I arose, taking with me a new consciousness which had, within it, gratitude for life itself. For the first time I began to understand the principles of free will, of choice. The need to blame God for what was, ended. It was replaced by courage to be God within, to take decision, to live, to be and to take responsibility for that. I began to see the difference between God's Will and humanity's will, to choose God's Will and embody the principles of Love and Brotherhood, to let go of fear and hatred and I ran and ran, hysterical with the joy of the gift of life, in full gratitude.

After a time I met again with the eyes of the full- bodied Sri Lankan man who had pointed me in the direction of the beach. I could see God in his eyes. I could see a need and a trust. He approached. I quickly related what had happened to me. He heard. He already knew, as it had happened to others before. He pleaded me to report it so that the man could be stopped. I felt filled with purpose to stop such energies of hatred and power, to stop this darkness, this evil force. I could feel the strength within me, the desire for justice. I felt, within me, an integrity I'd never before known.

*   *   *

To know what is right is one thing, to convey it and have it honoured, another. No-one was interested in Justice, at least not Divine Justice. Everyone had their own motive for wanting to assist me. I attempted to maintain the purity of my motive within an energy of extreme corruption. I went together with Hillo, the Sri Lankan man, to report the crime. Josie was half asleep when I told her what had happened. The shock of what happened to me hit her hard. She stayed at the guesthouse. Together with Hillo, on the back of his motor scooter, I went to the police station. It reminded me of the gaol-houses I'd seen in the American Western movies; a concrete floor, a desk and a cell, iron bars enclosing a wooden slat bed which came out from the wall, held in place by chains. There was a man behind the desk writing. He peered up at me through his glasses while writing.

I began my story after Hillo had said some words in Sri Lankan to him by way of introduction. He hardly bothered to look up. It was not until some days later when the bruising came out that any credence was given to my truth. I became instead a good target for the sexual aberrations of those in the police force. When others weren't looking, they would in turn, poke their tongues out and make rude signs. I was dumbfounded. A white woman amongst black men, a good scapegoat and the reason given for the brutal attack on all the men in the surrounding village that the police had vendettas towards. For days I travelled with them in the jeep. We would stop, enter a house and I would be asked if this was the man. I would say, "No," and the man would be beaten up anyway, brutally, with a baton, before my eyes. After several days of this I began to weigh up the effects upon my sanity. It felt clear to me I needed to leave. I talked with Josie. The only way to the police station every day was on Hillo's motor scooter, so my days had been spent without her support, which I very much needed at that time. I felt a great relief when finally, together, Josie and I decided to leave. I had looked for Justice in man's law. It was not there.

At this point I began to understand another reality other than the reality I had lived in until now. I began to see the illusion in many of the ways I had taken for granted. Divinity began its call. I had been traumatised. Seeing the world through those eyes was painful indeed. I spent some time with Hillo before we left being desensitised to the touch of man. In his wisdom he saw the necessity for touch, on a human level, to allow me to stay connected to life and love. With no hint of harassment, just compassion and a loving heart, he gave much time and energy to my healing. When I was strong enough, and had had enough of the police scenario, I left, continuing the process on my own. Josie and I decided we would head for Aragum Bay.

Chapter 3

THE UNGRACIOUS TRAVELLER

July 27, Aragum Bay, SRI LANKA

I had begun to really enjoy my time rejuvenating, being one with nature, the ocean, the sun. As time went by the thought of war had almost disappeared from the horizon. My body was beginning to heal. People were beginning to stop asking me what had caused all the bruising. I had fought so hard in that battle that the muscles along my back seized up whenever I'd try to get up in the morning, so I would roll out of bed and get up on all fours. That behaviour, too, was beginning to change. Then, it began again.

6 p.m. Curfew. Martial Law was again introduced. Jerra and Trinko didn't arrive home that night. They had been shot. They were young fellows, teenage, and were the people who had been looking after my needs, and the needs of many others, in the guesthouse for the duration of my stay there. The radios were on, people sat silently in candle light. More and more imminent was the threat of death. The desire to escape grew strong. I planned it with friends - the buses, the times, the routes.

July 28, Badella

Josie and I were headed for Colombo on the bus. All the people on the train-line had been killed the night before and the train was not running. I could feel the tension rising in the air. Everyone was tight lipped as they sat on the bus. All of a sudden the bus stopped. A man got on. He went immediately up to a man in front of me and pulled him up violently from the seat. He hurried the man down the aisle, took him off the bus and beat him. The bus waited while this new man got back on. It left, flicking dust all over the man that was beaten, leaving him lying in the dirt. I was horrified. The beaten man was a Tamil. They had come from India during the British rule of Ceylon, now Sri Lanka. They provided cheap labour for the British in those times and were quite renowned for being hard working. When the British left they made up forty per cent of the workforce. In this war, the Sri Lankans wanted some of their territory back. It was difficult. Not so clear cut. There were also of course many mixed marriages, creating even further dilemmas in the country. People were forced to leave spouses. This man had been thrown off the bus because he had the wrong shaped nose. I found it quite incredible.

The bus journeyed towards a town called Badella. As it approached the town a large group of women and children headed off the bus. It stopped and everybody got off quickly, as the women and children yelled loud, panicking sounds in their own language. Although I didn't understand the words, I could read the energy and I quickly followed the band of fleeing people. We fled around the bend ahead and the reason the women had stopped the bus became very evident. There, in front of us was an incinerated bus. Within it were the incinerated bodies of its passengers. If not for the women, we would have been next. I could smell the flesh. I turned heel and ran quickly across the tea fields, Josie running after me. We exchanged glances - this was unbelievable. It felt as if we were in a movie. Gun shots were headed in our direction. I ran fast and was aware as I ran of the richness of the fields. The grass was lush green, the earth red, the sun beating down hard and the native people scurrying like rabbits. I ran through a hedge and came to a road. I stood in the middle of the road and saw, on one side, men in uniforms with guns ready for attack, lying behind parapets, hessian bags filled with sand. On the other side were much younger men, huddled together on the back of a truck, at least thirty of them. Their hands were filled with bottles , filled with petrol and rags. I looked both ways and saw that I was in the middle of a battleground. I caught a glimpse across the road of a few elder men who saw the shocked look upon my face. One approached, placed his hand upon my shoulder and said, "You're not meant to be here, this is war."

The irony! I had never seen the division of masculine and feminine energies in this way. At this time my awareness was heightened to it and I said to the man,

"Well take us out of here!"

By this time Josie and I were both in a state of disbelief at the striking paradoxes we were seeing. We went with the man and he tried to make a space for us amongst the women. Being white we were a threat. Finally we found a spot for ourselves at the Buddhist temple. We could not enter as we were women, so we curled up on the verandah. We spent the next few days hiding out on the hard cement floor, eating rice rations that were thrown from the trucks once each day, wrapped in newspaper and drinking tea that the monks shared with us. Food was scarce. Fear was rising. The terrorists were coming.

July 31st

They arrived in all their fullness and were just as terrifying as the word suggests. A Tamil family had been seeking refuge in the temple. The terrorists raped the woman, shot the child, then the husband, then the wife. This was the plan of attack, for not only this family but for all the families they destroyed. Hiding behind the verandah, I waited my turn. They had heard there were Australian women at the temple and they thought they could get their share of sexual amusement. A Sri Lankan man with the ability to speak good English approached and put the suggestion to me. My body froze re-awakening the memory of Trincomalee. I woke Josie who assured me we would not have to engage in such activity. I was grateful for the consciousness that her words gave me. I could see the way clear. We made up a story to enable our escape, that we would meet them in some time for we would have to prepare our bodies, and they would have to prepare the beds, so we could do it properly and in style. Having stalled for time we fled, only to be stopped by the High Priest who would not give us shelter as we were women. He placed a kuri knife in my hand and put us in a room with a monk and a European Sri Lankan who had attached himself to us, in order that he would not be likened to the Tamils. He was angry that we had made the terrorists angry and was full of fear and blame that we had somehow endangered his life by not complying with the terrorists' demands. I sat, bated breath, knife in hand, in the dark of the room and within a few moments, the monk had made a pass and the Sri Lankan European tried to steal my passport. I screamed! I had reached the limit of my endurance. My heart beat fast and even though there was curfew and the possibility of being shot in the streets, it seemed safer than where we were and together Josie and I decided to leave.

We passed bodies, piles of bodies burning, houses burning; the stench of burning flesh filled the air, omnipresent. People were looting. The futility and absurdity of war overwhelmed me. Rumours came that the train was still stopped, no buses were leaving the town. I began to feel empty, too empty to be angry, too empty to be sad. Distraught, wondering, "Where was God?" If there was not fear in the eyes of those I met, there was a vacancy. People had left. No one was there. I was alone. Tears formed and poured down my face, I could not feel them, my face was numb.

And then I remembered, "I am God and I have choice and I choose life!" I went to the bus station. I demanded that a bus be released to take me and the others here out of this war town. They had rules, `You must have a bus conductor and a driver!' I found them. `You must have a piece of paper signed by the man in charge.' It was 6 a.m., the man in charge was not coming until 9 o'clock. This seemed absurd, that even in war, people kept their regular times and arrived with briefcase and neatly pressed trousers and shirts in brown tones. With vacant eyes that looked incapable of making a decision, the man in charge arrived. I approached his office and pleaded with him, appealing to his sense of humanity. I was not sure it was there, but I probed deeply and asked him to release a bus, that some may have the chance of survival.

Within five minutes the bus was released. The driver drove the bus as if it were a motorbike. It was jammed full of people, clinging to the seats and to the rafters, not knowing whether it would be hit by a petrol bomb or guns, not knowing whether it would make it out of town. All within the bus united in with prayer and hope, with an overriding sense of mortality. The journey took some thirteen hours. I arrived in Colombo to see a city destroyed by bombs, crows eating bodies on the side walks and men in uniform dotted around the streets were the only sign of human life.

Within the walls of the buildings it was a different story, human life was buzzing, people gathered around watching news broadcasts, I watched too. The local news showed a totally different story from the news which went abroad. The newspaper showed a different story from what I had seen that day. The headline read, "Violence Diminishes" and yet violence was rife in every direction I had looked. I had entered a large hotel complex earlier that day.

Because I had not looked clean (I had been in the rural war zone for some days and had no access to water or food, except for the rice rations) those in the hotel decided I was not good enough custom. I was asked to leave. I was appalled at this, mainly because there was shooting and fire outside and I was pushed out into it. The hypocrisies loomed large in my consciousness and again I looked at the world through traumatised eyes. My awareness was heightened by the inner suffering and pain. I passed some tourists, who were complaining about the lack of food and the lack of fun for their four weeks' vacation from Germany. I felt sick. I could see the reflection of what I myself had been like, as an ungracious traveller, out for what I could get rather than what I could give.

I had felt on several occasions now that I would die in this country. I began to see that it was time to leave, for lesson upon lesson had come my way awakening me to a new set of values and understandings. I could see that it was a gift of experience, necessary to rid myself of outmoded values and attitudes of selfishness and self-centredness, to broaden my perspective and to bring forth my compassion, to make me see the illusion of man's reality and to help me to look deeper for the Divine in all. I had wondered before this, why, if there was a God, that God could allow such destruction and evil to take place. I could see now, that it is here that the free will of humanity comes into play. It is one of the Divine Laws that Christ cannot interfere unless we call. I could no longer be angry or blame God for what mankind has done. The absence of God or the presence of God is up to humanity.

Together with a number of others I paid a taxi driver a lot of money to go through the war ridden city of Colombo. On arrival at the airport I saw people coping with this war, with their situation, in different ways. There was much use of alcohol and drugs. Many had found instead a depth of creativity, people were painting, drawing, listening to music, all waiting for flights that may not come for days. Planes entered, emptied, left full, and travellers lent money to strangers, without knowing that it would be repaid. I could see that the suffering brought understanding and wisdom to many and sent others over the edge. There were lessons and there was choice as to whether one opened one's eyes to these lessons or not. Life is full of that, it seems. I parted company with Josie who flew to another city. I wondered why we had shared this time when both of us felt so alone.

Chapter 4

THE POWER OF PRAYER

I couldn't return to the Western world, certainly not home. I thought no one would understand. I didn't understand and I had to process it. I had to spend time with it. Even though I'd had certain insights, understandings and recognitions, certain senses of the Divine, I had to let them integrate into my being a little longer. My body was full of trauma, even though Hillo had spent some time helping me de-sensitise.

I flew to Thailand which was more Western than Sri Lanka and it somehow formed a bridge for me. Bangkok, a busy modern city represented that bridge with its fast pace of city life, and materialism in full swing, it was enough to distract me from the raw core I had gone to in the East in Sri Lanka. I spent some time there with others who had also been affected by the war. We had met on the plane and we huddled together throughout our stay in Bangkok, until we were able to process some of the effects. When time was right, we left one another grateful for the sharing, continuing our own journeys to many different parts of the world.

I went to London, hoping to be inspired by Western thought. I was headed to the Fringe Festival held in Scotland. There I found the intellect for which I was looking. It took some time to re-educate my being to Western habit - little things like walking along the streets that were paved with bitumen and cement, footpaths with no pot-holes or rocks on which to stumble. I remember flying into Copenhagen Airport on the way to London. Here the contrast was phenomenal. Everything was shining clean. The people were blonde and blue eyed, not small and dark as in the East. I was in transition. I knew I had to go with it. I was not yet ready to return to my own country. There was more to understand.

I went to Edinburgh which was abuzz with little coffee shops, people trendily dressed; strangely dressed in my eyes, very little colour. There were vegetarian restaurants humming all over the town. Plays, theatre, films were on everywhere. Every possible venue was utilised. Here were people who thought about things. Here was I thinking about what was happening to me, the world and my place in it. The parallel was appropriate. I was trying to make sense of life. I went to different plays in the day and night hoping to find something within them to parallel me, or crack the shell that was around me. In my body I was going through much trauma. I noticed especially the lack of touch in the Western world. The density of population, the culture itself was very different when travelling in the East. The number of people jostling around in the bus, the crowds in the ticket queues, ensured touch. Here, because I didn't know anyone, it was possible to go without touch for months on end. In my state I found it difficult to reach out. It was affecting me internally.

I didn't menstruate and I was afraid. It frightened me that I might have a child under such circumstances. One of the plays I had seen was called "Abortion Tapes." In it a variety of scenes were enacted depicting the dreams women had had following abortions; white masked men, scenes of death and drowning. I felt horrified. I kept having pregnancy tests. The result was always negative. When I stood up from that beach in Sri Lanka I prayed to God very hard and very loud, "Please, just one thing I ask, don't let me be pregnant from this." I was not even sure that he was able to penetrate me as all my energy was going into the fight for life itself. Nonetheless, I was concerned. After every test, every negative result, I became more and more sure that I wouldn't be let down. God was growing within me. I'd seen God in the sun, in Hillo's eyes. Indeed, in a few people's eyes since. The heart, the soul, the love, all this was growing within me as though a seed was being born. It was growing in my perception of the world; a new consciousness, a resurrection.

I spent only a short time amid the Western thought and began to yearn again for the east. Not the East of Sri Lanka, the east of the Himalayas. East, where the people, their warmth and smiles of the heart, come inside you as you greet them along the streets. I yearned for that. At the same time I felt I should go somewhere whilst in Europe before I returned to the East. I went to Holland.

Amsterdam seemed beautiful to me. It gave me another view of Western life. There was something about the people and the place. I liked it, it had heart. The streets had much character, the architecture had character. The canals in the streets, the funny little cars, the Dutch way of dress, all had colour and life. There were lots of bicycles. It was clear there was culture and a depth of wisdom in the lifestyle. I visited Van Goghs's Gallery and felt the life in the pictures come inside me, with all its eccentricities. I pondered on what it would be like to bring that brilliance into form, into life. I could feel the passion and the love in the strokes. The colours I loved and the simplicity of the scenes appealed to me a great deal.

The day I visited the gallery I wandered home, riding my hired bicycle along the cobblestone streets, over little bridges, along the tree lined lanes and back to the Youth Hostel where I was staying. I had planned to go out to dinner that evening with some girls I had met. One was called Suzanne and came from California. The other couple were French and did not speak much English. I talked mainly to Suzanne. We went to a restaurant in the main

street and ordered mussels. They came with a bucket load. I'd never experienced that before. So many! We began to eat. The French couple struck up a conversation with each other. Suzanne and I began to talk about ourselves. It was the first real opportunity I had had, for some time, or had allowed myself to connect with another. I told her what had happened to me in Sri Lanka and to my surprise she was quite amazed at my story. She told me I should pray. The words seemed strong and impossible, something alien to my understanding. It resounded in my head for days afterwards.
I told her, "I don't know how to."

She said, "I will help you. All you have to do is want to and I'll help."

"I don't know if I want to," I said, "I don't know what it is."

We let it rest but I thought about it a lot of the time. It felt like something I had once had connection with and had lost. I found it difficult to comprehend.

More and more as time went on in Amsterdam I found it difficult to find the joy in living. I was meeting many people, seeing new things but a new yearning began. I wanted to go home to my own country, to my own people. The day came for me to leave the hostel. An hour before I was due to leave to catch the bus to France something clicked inside me and I went down to Suzanne and said to her, "I want to pray, will you help me?"

She said that she could help tomorrow.

"I leave in an hour." I said.
"Just a minute." she said. Within five minutes she returned with someone ready to take over her job, she was on reception. She took

26

me upstairs to a little room. I went into the room with her. It was an odd room, it had lots of old boxes and things in it, books. It seemed a bit like a storeroom. We found ourselves a space within it and sat down. She took my hand and said to me,

"Say what I say, after me."

We began. "I call upon the Lord Jesus and ask you Lord to come into my heart, to have mercy on me....". There were many more words but I do not remember them for as I spoke something very beautiful happened. I felt myself disappear and turn into Light. Everything was white. I felt huge and tiny at the same time. My eyes were flickering. Everything in the room disappeared, she disappeared, I could no longer feel her hand. I felt instead this incredible pain. I knew it was my pain. I cried deep, deep tears from the middle of my stomach, yet everything else was Light. When I looked ahead I could see a tiny, tiny vision, a little speck. As I looked closely I could see it was a vision of the Lord Jesus. It made me cry more to see this. It turned into Light, as I and everything around me was Light, moving towards infinity in every direction. Some minutes later, it seemed, my vision of the room returned, of Suzanne holding my hand. I heard her thank the Lord for what she had witnessed and for the mercy He had shown. It all seemed like a strange language to me and I wasn't sure of what to make of what had happened. She put a Bible in my hand and told me it would be my guide.

"You'd better go or you'll miss your bus."
I said, "It's okay, it comes in an hour."

She said, "No, it is waiting downstairs, we've been here an hour." I looked at the clock and could see she was telling the truth. I hadn't experienced time in that way, not that I could remember. It

27

added to my confusion. I ran downstairs and as I headed towards the bus I heard her yelling, "It's all right, just look in the Bible when you need help!"

"Did that really happen?" I thought. I didn't know what to make of it. I made my way into the bus and sat next to a girl who was sleeping. I closed my eyes and did the same and woke up in France.

*   *   *

I sat under the Eiffel Tower with my knapsack. The sun was shining and thousands of pigeons were flying around, just as I expected France would be. I had a bread roll and some cheese - that was the thing to do in France, eat the bread and cheese. I noticed the age of the buildings around me. They were older and dirtier than I thought they would be. I could feel the culture in the air, the thoughts, the passions that had gone before. I was staying in a little apartment in St. Michele. I liked the little streets at night and the sidewalk cafes. After some days though, the yearning for going home returned. It was a strange world this Western one, with all its politics and intellectual thought, its emphasis on economy. There was still, within it, elements of being-ness. You could see it in the eyes of the people in the parks, the artists on the streets, the people playing music in the subway. Some of them had it. Some had instead a hunger, a thirst, a need, evident in the vacancy of their eyes and the sallowness of their skin, the anaemic colour of blood itself. I could feel this duality in me.

The desire to return home was growing stronger. I wasn't really sure where home was any more. I felt, within me, a need to return to the East. I did. I stopped in Indonesia on the way home. When I stopped I planned to be there a few days. The love of humanity in those I met made me decide to stay longer. I arrived at the airport and went through customs as usual. It was a little airport, a beach airport. There were many people from many nations stopping here for a holiday. It was a good holiday spot and many had the idea of laying in the sun, swimming in the seas, going snorkelling, going to the mountains. Many people, many purposes. I walked up to the baggage claim area and waited. An hour later I was still waiting and so were several other people from the same flight. By this stage we began to talk. I'd noticed a girl who I thought was very beautiful. She had a New Zealand accent, radiant eyes and was very pretty. She was speaking to all the people around. Her words sounded like music. She had a guitar strapped over her shoulder. As we were waiting she sat down and began to play. I'd said a prayer earlier (I was getting better at it),

"Please, let me meet people who believe in God."

Much of my life had been spent with those who did not, in a void of reverence. Her songs were of love and peace in the world. I looked at her and said, "Your words are very beautiful." Her teeth gleamed as she smiled and her face lit up.

Her eyes met mine, "I'm Veronica," she said. "Are you alone too?"
"Yes."
"Perhaps we could share some time."

There was another girl not far away who looked a little like we did. Similar age, a spark in the eyes. She smiled at the two of us.

"Would you like to join us too?"
"Yes, I'll be in that. I've had enough time on my own." she said.

We had a special time together, the three of us. We spent several days together, sometimes the three of us, sometimes two of us,

29

sometimes alone. We shared a lot of our experiences, all of us having travelled for some time. It felt like sisters returning home after the school term for vacations, sharing all the exploits of what happened at school. We talked and talked and talked, sharing our feelings and thoughts about life in general, men and women. I felt myself thawing out. I could speak to them about anything and everything. We even talked about God, all of us considering the possibility of God's existence. I knew my prayers had been answered. I was meeting those who did, somewhere in them, believe.

I found a great deal of joy in the simple things again; the sand, the sun, the nature, the palm trees, the beauty of the country, the colour of the flowers, the garments the women wore, the smiles, the wisdom of the older women, the beauty of the food, its delicate tastes and variety, and all the sounds and smells of Asia which I loved. My friends went home, I stayed back because I wanted to savour life here for a little longer. I wanted to bring it into me in order to heal the shocks that I had experienced. I wanted to know life was worth living, that there was beauty in simplicity. I stayed another month. I moved to the middle of the island and rented a house in the palm trees, in the rice fields; a very simple house. I could eat breakfast, go for walks in the rice fields, read, write and converse with those I met in my daily existence. I contemplated life, a simple existence, preparing me for my journey home.

Chapter 5

LETTING GO

March 4, 1984 Melbourne

I woke at 6 a.m. breathless. Breath was very difficult to get. I had a nebuliser* that helped me to get oxygen and ventolin into my lungs when I was finding it difficult to breathe. I'd had asthma before. This particular morning the machine wasn't working. Fortunately, a close friend, Paul, came and insisted on taking me to hospital. He went downstairs where there were policemen booking some people, outside in the street. An interesting coincidence for he did not know where the hospitals were in Melbourne, being new to Australia. Paul, an American, had only been in the country a few weeks. I had met him some months earlier in Bali. The policeman came up the stairs followed by Paul. I was blacking in and out of consciousness. I remember being taken downstairs. It was very difficult to breathe. My full concentration was on breath. My body swelled when I had asthma in this way. I felt uncomfortable with clothing and wore a sloppy shirt and trousers.. When I sat in the police van and the siren went I could feel myself completely letting go. On the one hand I knew if there was any hope for life, it would be forthcoming. If I was to die that would happen too, I felt little attachment to the outcome.

The next thing I knew I was placed on a table in the hospital. There were mechanical attachments being placed upon my chest area. Both lungs had collapsed, the air blown throughout my body causing my eyes to be closed from the swelling. There was a short time, forty five seconds as I later discovered, when my brain received no oxygen before they placed me on the life support machine. I had died.

I felt myself leaving my body through a tunnel. Going up the tunnel, I was surrounded by white light and felt an infinite love all through me until I became One with the light and the love. I could sense that that was all there is. This felt like home, the home I'd wanted to come to and had been searching for for some time.

A movie screen appeared and lifetimes flashed before me that I could recognise as my own. I had never really given credence to the idea of reincarnation. When I was being shown it in this state of consciousness, its reality loomed large. There was no doubt as to its reality. In one of the scenes, in my perception the walls of the hospital turned into a mud like substance, mud brick, not the plaster that they were in this world sense of time and place. The Doctor that I had, although Scandinavian looking in this lifetime, appeared to be of a German nature. I felt also that I was not Cheryl but someone else and that an experiment was being performed on me. It became very clear to me that I was in Germany and my name wasn't Cheryl.

I saw myself in a series of lifetimes in which I played the victim role, where I was dependent on others, or at least that is how I felt my role was in them. I kept watching these images trying to make sense of them and I kept asking within, what is this, why am I seeing this. The answers began to come.

"It is because you do not trust enough. You must let people be close to you. In former times this lack of trust has lead to disease with you and you have died through a lack of touch. Don't let it happen this time. Learn the lesson of trust, open your heart and let people in."

I could see that I really was in a position where I had to trust. It was presently being tested. My hands were bound up and I had machines attached all over me. Catheters and tubes were placed in me and down my throat. I was in the Intensive Care ward, very much at the mercy of the doctors and nurses. I could see the sense of what was being shown to me. I saw not just the past but the future. The necessity of learning this lesson began to enter me, the knowing came at the body level. This was truth.

As far as medical records were concerned, I had cerebral amnesia and for several days. I had been on a life support machine which was oxygenating my blood. As far as I was concerned this supposed state of unconsciousness was the most conscious I had ever been. On the seventh day I started to take some breaths.

The Awakening

Chapter 6

HOME

April 17th 1984

The nurse came to the room to get me ready. I was very excited for it was the first time I was to go out into the world. Dressed in my blue hospital gown I moved across into the wheelchair, helped by the orderlies, who were there to help the nurse.

"Are you ready Cheryl?"

"Yes." I said, full of anticipation. I felt exhilarated by all the events that were happening to me. I had come to feel very at home in the hospital and got used to the routine. It all seemed familiar, the corridors, the light brown tiles, the cream walls, the patients in blue gowns, the steel of the wheel chairs, the blood pressure machine, the thermometers. I knew it well, I had explored even as far as the physio room where I could bicycle for one and a half minutes. I had been building up to that for weeks.

It was a sunny day outside I was told. I might like to get some fresh air. I had been granted permission to go out into the park across the road. The nurse's name was Sylvia, and I had come to like her. She had a hardy disposition and a good sense of humour. We began our journey along the corridors. I saw many people I knew as we moved along the corridors and down the lift. I had found my way around and familiarised myself with every aspect of this place. I seemed to have within me now a very strong love of life, a fascination with people, a love in my heart and a will to do good. The aluminium framed doors opened as we approached the mat which signalled the doors to do so. I could feel a real difference in the air. I had grown accustomed to air conditioning. The breath of wind and the density of air was something quite different. We crossed the busy road and moved into the park which extended as far as my eyes could see. There were huge trees and green grass, people walking with children, with dogs, men playing cricket, birds chirping.

With every breath I took I felt myself become more and more exhilarated by the love of life. I began to cry tears of joy, for the beauty I could see in the world.

"This is Heaven." I thought and I felt it too, within me.
"It's here. It's been here all the time."

The tears streamed down for quite a long time. I felt mesmerised. I could see the life in the atoms in the air, everything seemed to be in a white mist. This experience of Light had begun to come with more frequency since that time in Holland and especially since this death experience with the collapsed lungs. I would spend hours in a meditative state experiencing the brilliance of the love and light that surrounded me and filled me. I felt blessed with an incredible will to live and love.

Because of the tubes down my throat during the time of the intensive care I did not have full voice capacity, so I would often sit and observe without speaking. When I did communicate I would either write it down or need to have the full attention of the person to whom I was speaking. I could feel a real sense of immediacy within me. When I spoke with others I tried to help them see and have gratitude for life itself, as I did. I felt almost evangelical.

I had been reborn. I was different. I knew. I remember the feelings clearly, of being a vehicle of Light, a soul and I felt for the first time that I was not my body. I could feel that I was something much more than that. I was not my mind nor my emotions, I was soul. This contact I had never had before. I felt as if I had a mission, a purpose; to awaken people to the Love and Light that is here on Earth for us to find, that lies within us if we look.

I sat looking at my body, my arms, my legs, I was fascinated by the way they were designed, that the little fingers fitted in to the ears and the nose. In time I would get it to walk again. I gathered strength and momentum of purpose. I found home at last, in my own heart, I knew that no matter where I was in the world, or in what circumstances I found myself, to feel the sense of home all I had to do, was go within and find the light and love of the heart. I felt ready to do whatever was required. I asked within. The answer came,

"Learn to love your body. Come to know and love yourself. That is your first task."

When my voice returned I would know what to say to people. I was observing and learning. I had to come to terms with how people had seen me in the past. I was aware that I was not the same any more and it would take time for others and me to adjust to and know this change. I was given that time in the hospital and for some months afterwards to do just that. The journey was just beginning.

Chapter 7

SYNTHESIS

July 1984

It was a beautiful, sunny Saturday. It was lovely to have time to myself to do whatever I pleased. I had the afternoon free. I heard there was a psychic fair on at the showgrounds. I had never been to such a thing before. The title and the idea of it appealed to me. There were a lot of people there, I was told, who had stalls and things to do with a new way of thinking, a new Age. I was becoming more and more interested in this. I had recently started a job in the Findhorn bookshop, where there were many books about many topics in which I was extremely interested. They seemed to contain ways of thinking I hadn't yet thought about, ways of looking at and seeing the world I hadn't yet perceived. I was fascinated and loved the voluntary job. I had come across it quite by accident and was very happy to be able to do that with part of my week. It also helped me to gain insight into ways I could go about my healing. Through these books I could see the need to look after myself in order to then give to others. This I knew was my task, to learn to come to know myself. This was the task I set myself.

I organised to go to this fair with some girlfriends. They were very happy to come along. I felt very happy to be able to go out with some friends for the afternoon. I arrived at the building and went inside. There were stalls everywhere, all sorts, with beautiful music and a pleasant atmosphere with very soft, instrumental music that was very calming to the nerves and the mind. The colours of things were also very beautiful, soft, pastel shades that

41

felt good to have around me. I wandered from stall to stall and met many interesting and fascinating people.

I came to one stall where a woman held a silver rod in her hand, with crystals attached to the end of it. People were lining up and she was waving the rod in a peculiar fashion around them. I asked someone what was happening. They told me she was cleansing the aura. I knew a little about the aura from what I had read in books. I understood it had something to do with our connection to the spiritual world. I stood in line and stood before her. I began to feel a field of Light around me and became aware of strange sensations and of feelings that reminded me of the energies I had felt in Holland when I had called on Lord Jesus to enter into my heart, and the feelings I had in the hospital. She directed me to a chair. A girl was standing behind me. As I sat a bolt of Light came down through me. I recognised the energy. It was the same, it was the Christ energy. I knew it was. I was shocked. Here, these people were sending that Light of the Christ into me. I could sense there was more for me to understand.

I discovered that the lady who had given me the aura cleansing had established a School of Healing and Wisdom in Melbourne. I joined and later came to know this lady as Lady Shan Tara. She taught me a great deal and I began to understand many things and gain much knowledge about the spiritual world. It all linked into my own experience, and went beyond it. I began to see that many people on earth had experiences as I had. Many had come to new understandings in many different ways about Light and Love, about the heart. I began to be very interested in Theosophical thought. These things I had never considered seriously before. It started for me a process of much learning. I was very interested. I started, also, to experience many new things in the field of spirit, this world of Light. It was for me the start of bringing that Light to earth, bringing that experience on the inner planes that I had with the Christ energy into my life in fullness, to make it visible, tangible and practical and help me in my day to day existence in my life on earth.

Chapter 8

GOING UP

I sat with Mary in the lounge-room, pleased at this new discovery; a method through which I could talk to my Higher-self* when I wanted. It seemed all I had to do was allow an image to come and talk with it. Provided I was pure in my motive I would get answers that I could sense were part of my Higher nature. They really did help me a lot and gave a lot of help and guidance on matters of a personal and spiritual nature.

Mary was as excited about all this new learning as I was. We were sharing a house and had come to know each other quite well through our discoveries in this new world. We had learned this process together at a workshop that weekend and had decided to spend the evening practising our new skills. It was like doing a surprise jigsaw puzzle with the mind. You could never really tell what would come next or what picture it would make. By the end it always made sense and had a beauty of its own.

It was about eight o'clock. We had done the dishes together and talked about our day with the others with whom we lived; we shared the house with another woman, Rosette and her two daughters. I was very much enjoying the time we spent sharing. I could hear the girls outside in the passage giggling as Rosette attempted to get them to bed. Mary and I began. I asked for an image to come forward.

A man appeared with an aboriginal face. He felt warm and I felt as though I could trust him. He also had a sense of urgency about him.

45

"There is work for you to do" he said. I could feel that he meant it.

"What sort of work?" I was aware as I responded that whatever it was he asked of me I would do, there was something very trustworthy about him. I was a little surprised to find myself so trusting in this. It was a new and beautiful quality I was discovering.

"There is work to be done on the land to redeem some things that your ancestors have done. Some healing is needed with the nature spirits to balance karma and bring healing to the earth."

I couldn't quite comprehend how I could help in such a task, but I felt honoured and I asked the man to be more specific. I was surprised at what then unfolded. A friend of mine had been having trouble selling his land. He had a farm in Mudgigonga.

"You can help your friend."

"How?" As I asked I was shown a tree. There was a cut in the tree in the shape of a woman. Sap was pouring out and I could sense the tree was in pain.

"You must heal the tree; find it, send it Light. You must take five large candles, the type that burn for days, some incense and plenty of cleaning equipment. You must go with your friend to the farm and tell him that your task is to cleanse it. I will tell you more when you arrive. I will see you then." With that, he disappeared.

It was all new to me, this sort of connection and clarity of communication. The trust was there. I was learning about faith, trust and courage. I told my friend, Flower, the news some days later. He worked at Findhorn with me some days, selling tapes, books and crystals, and some days he worked there alone. I knew that day I could catch him if I went by the shop. I told him exactly what I had been told by the aborigine. He was not at all surprised.

"That figures. What about next weekend?" he said.

I couldn't understand why he was not surprised and I asked him about the tree.

"There was an aborigine, a young lad whom I had staying on the land up at the farm for some years. He arrived, had no money and lived off the land. At one time he took to himself a Californian girlfriend. They shared a close time and she left to go home to her homeland. He did not want her to go. He was angry. With that anger he carved a picture of her into the tree. I have seen it. I couldn't tell you exactly where it is, there are ninety acres of bush on the farm, but I'm sure if you're meant to find it and heal it, you will."

We organised the time and space to go to the farm that next weekend. On the Friday night he arrived to pick me up. I was quite excited to be going to the country. Armed with candles, incense, blankets and food, we began our journey, heading up the highway, away from the city. It was beautiful to be out on the open country road. There was something I liked too about driving at night. Even though it was dark I could sense the bush around us.

After about an hour we stopped for a counter meal and shared and chatted a lot about our past and our lives. I remember when I first met Flower we were going up in an elevator. He was in a suit. He looked very distinguished. It was my first day at a new job where I was to be working as an interviewer for the Road Traffic Authority. I had imagined that Flower had been there forever and attributed to him all the qualities of a stable businessman. Little did I know. It was his first day too, and we would be working together, not only in this job but at Findhorn as well. When we met in the elevator we both said simultaneously, "Going up?" Those words somehow represented our relationship over the coming months. We spent quite a deal of time together and I always felt that when we were together there was an energy about it that took us up in consciousness. Very shortly after we left the elevator we found ourselves facing each other, seated at desks. Here, we were to enjoy many a long conversation. It was quite a pleasant gift the universe gave us. We had much to share about healing and other things of common interest. I was very aware we had been together before. We finished our counter meal and headed off on the journey again. Another couple of hours in close proximity in the car enabled us to share and get close.

I was quite exhausted by the time we arrived. It seemed the farm at Mudgigonga was at the end of nowhere. We passed huge trees and landmarks, pot holes in the road, dirt tracks and finally ended up pulling into a rickety old car-port. The farm was completely different from what I had imagined. It was much smaller and much more run down. There were things everywhere, junk, bits of old metal, bits and pieces of lamps and televisions, pieces of plastic and old tins of paint. We walked across towards the house itself. I was quite exhausted and thought only of getting into bed and sleeping.

There was no light. The candles came in very handy. When I lit them I was shocked at what I saw. The place was a mess. It smelt, it was filthy. I began to look around. On the wall, to my amazement, was a picture of the aborigine who had come to me as my guide. He had an elderly face. As I saw the painting I heard the words in my head,

"I told you I would meet you when you arrived." I sat down in front of it.

"You will have to begin the cleansing now or you will find it impossible to stay here. Be calm and just go about it systematically."

Flower entered the room. I was looking at the picture and I said to him,

"Where did you get this?"
"It was painted for me twenty years ago by a psychic woman. She said that he was my guide."

I looked up at him. "It's the same face as the man who sent me here, that guide I told you about."

His eyes communicated a look of recognition, "Yes, I thought as much."

I looked around the room and saw that there was much to be done. I decided I would take courage and began to open the doors and explore the rest of the house.

"What's in there?" I pointed to one of the bedrooms.
"It was my daughter's room." He said.

I went towards the door and opened it. I felt a shock wave go through my body. In the middle of the room was a doll sitting up, just as they sometimes show them in the horror movies. As I saw it a rat ran across the room. I squealed and closed the door quickly. I felt I could only look in that room in the morning in the light. I asked Flower if there was any way the rat could get out and I became aware that there was not one rat but many. I lit the candles, lit the incense and called upon all the protection I could muster, all of the help on the inner levels I could find. Very late in the evening I fell asleep, curled up on the couch, a little comforted by the burning candles. I was very glad that I had brought the ones that burned for days. I knew I needed them.

The day broke and as I awoke I saw Flower in front of me sitting in a chair, reading. He could have been there all night for all I knew. The candles were burning and there was a sweet smell in the house. The energy felt very different from the night before. Still, I could not blow out the candles. I began physically cleaning, sweeping, wiping benches, while Flower prepared my breakfast. When I was finished I walked outside. The beauty of the land greeted me. I could hear the birds and the Australian bush calling and see the mists on the trees and the ground. It felt so beautiful to be out of the city and in this wonderland of nature. For the first time I could sense and feel the love Flower had when he had been talking about his land. When I had seen only the house the night before I found it difficult to comprehend his love for this place. I breathed in the air and took it within. I could sense aeons of time where others before me had stood and breathed in the air and felt the beauty, the Nature. There were lots of rewards for doing the work the inner provides us with to do. I put on my gumboots and raincoat and went into the bush.

I had an eerie feeling as I walked. There were bones on the ground, animal bones, everywhere I looked. I kept walking, thinking about the land, the nature and man's part in community with nature. I asked to be guided as I went. I was looking for the tree. I sat down on a rock to meditate.

The face of the aborigine appeared again. "There are a couple of trees. Head North and you will find them, past the water-hole."

I could not find a water-hole but I headed north and after some twenty minutes found the water-hole and came to a tree with sap coming out of it. The markings were clear. I felt as though I could feel the pain of the tree and found myself asking the nature spirit of the tree for forgiveness for what my ancestors and other humans on the earth had done.

"Send Golden Light, call upon the Angels of Light and ask that the tree be healed."

I did this and witnessed the most beautiful Light descending into the tree. It lit up before my eyes, golden energy moving up and down the tree to infinity. I saw violet Light as well. I hugged the tree. I felt One with it and knew the work had been done. As I was walking back I saw another tree with the markings of a man engraved in it, obviously done by the same person. I followed the same process with it and again witnessed glorious Light.

I walked back towards the house feeling that something more had to be done. There was a cluster of rocks, very large ones. I clambered up them. As I stood at the top Flower came along. He had an odd energy about him.

"What is it? You seem a bit disturbed."
"It's my father. I'm angry at him and I don't know what to do about it."
"You're father is dead isn't he?" I asked.
"Yes. He haunts me."

As I looked at Flower I could see that he seemed different in his character and stature. I felt that I could sense his father in his being.

"What is it you feel you've done wrong." I said.

"I feel guilty about this land, that it was taken from the aborigines and used in such a cold way."

"What are the bones?" I asked.

"Goats," he said," I slaughtered them all."

I could feel his pain. He had slaughtered them to get them off his land. He said he didn't know what else he could do. What happened then was rather a lengthy process. Together we processed feelings which Flower had about the goats and his father until we came to a point where together we prayed for the forgiveness of our ancestors and ourselves for what had been done to the land and the animal life in the name of mankind. We went back to the house and I could feel that much of the work I had come to do had been completed.

We still had one day left. We cooked a beautiful meal that evening. I could feel my senses being satisfied after the hours it took to create the meal, chopping wood, lighting the stove. I could feel the contrast between the food we ate then and the food that is cooked in an electric or gas oven in city life. There was something about every morsel that touched every tastebud. The moments of time we shared held that quality also, every moment mattered, every word spoken meant something. I remembered the Himalayas.

While we were talking that evening I picked up a stone. It had been painted. I held it and looked into it. It seemed as if it contained the entire history and future of mankind. As I watched I saw the movie within it. It went from aeons past to millions of years hence. I saw everything that was, is and will be in that stone. I asked Flower if I could have it. I had never experienced anything like it. He laughed. There was no way I could take it for it belonged to the land. I had to let go of it and let things be.

By the time we were ready to go the next day I felt as though I had been there a month. That one weekend taught me many things. As we journeyed home across the open country road towards the city I asked within that I be able to hold on to the consciousness that I had found; finding meaning in every moment, being. I was grateful for the opportunity to learn in such a beautiful way. I thanked the aborigine and returned to my home in the city.

The next week when I met Flower he told me the farm had been sold.

It seemed difficult in the West. There was not the perennial quality of spirit that I had felt in the country in the East. I felt instead a more intermittent experience of spirit, coloured by the lifestyle I led and the fast pace of the Western world. Life became split in a way and the discrepancy between the more 'holy' part of my being and my lower nature became more and more evident. During the days I would sometimes sink into vagueness and in the evenings and on Sundays I would experience intense connection with spirit, sometimes when alone and sometimes when I would go along to be a part of the group spiritual activities taking place. It seemed the integration of spirit took time. The discrepancy was heightened by the contrasting lifestyle and the anonymity which I had through living in a city with four million people. Within such an environment it was easy for me to satisfy all the parts of my character. For many city life offers that opportunity. The process was gradual. I felt within me that desires were becoming aspiration instead. Some of what I had experienced in the Himalayas was beginning to come back into my consciousness. I was yearning for that purity of mind and heart that I had found there. In the dense vibration of the city, with all its hustle and bustle and its mundaneness, I found it hard to find, my own nature vibrating with the denseness of the roads and concrete, my spirit yearning to vibrate with the trees and birds.

The intensity and heights of spirit to which I rose at night seemed almost like a drug to me. It lured me. I felt a huge part of my being pulled towards it like a magnet. Parts of my character that were frightened of the vibration of spirit began to shake. They had no choice but to fall away. It was the only possible outcome. Slowly the alignment took place. People, places, habits, ways of being, one by one fell away. Anger, resentment, sentimentality, fear and guilt began to loosen their hold upon me. The hardest part of it all was having to see them and feel them as they did - to learn forgiveness, to not blame or rebel, to move out of the role of victim, to lose the idea of revenge and the chance of being the oppressor - all of these I had to feel in order that I might let them go. I began to realise that if I wanted to feel the purity of heart within me, I first had to know and experience all of me that wasn't that. I had to meet the reality of the shadow within.

Chapter 9

OPENING TO LOVE

I had experienced great Light within me and still found battle within myself. My shadow was becoming more evident. I would have thought that with the experiences I had in Light, this shadow would somehow dissipate. But that was not to be. For the shadow needed to be understood, recognised and embraced, in order that I might move into spirit in truth. Opening to love was not easy. Many fears seemed to get in the way. Even though I had made a conscious decision to open, there were many things lurking in my unconscious that were stopping me. I had to look more deeply.

I closed my eyes and I could see it. The tears began streaming down my face for I had begun to know the pain of the past. I could see myself standing by a window, looking out. I was in a Tudor type cottage in England, a well-to-do place. I was dressed in well to do clothes, lace cuffs, velvet bodice. I could feel deep pain within. I was leaving the house where I lived with my father whom I loved dearly. He was dead. I had taken his head off the pike from the Tower of London where it had been placed after his execution. I brought it home. I did not think it should be there for all to see. I placed it in a box. I did not want the King to have it. I was angry and bitter. I could not see why my father should die for a principle, like others before him had died, friends of mine also. They, too, were beheaded. I had felt great love in this life. I could feel it now, a passion deep within. The pain and the hurt about the betrayal I felt when my father was killed and the loss of those I loved caused me to lose the will to live. I could do little now but express my anger and bitterness. I could not stay in the house. I had to move. I went to the court and from then on challenged every decision made. I was angry at all the ideals for the loss they had caused me, but I stood up to them for my father's sake, flying his flag for the depth of my love for him. This was so real. I could feel many things within in terms of my relationships with others at this time. I was not very happy in my marriage. I had lived only for my father. We shared an intensity of relationship that stimulated my mind and heart. I was angry at God because my father had died for God, in God's name. I was angry at the principles.

My eyes opened. I was in the twentieth century and yet I felt as though I were a person from the past. It was all so real. I felt another identity as strong within me as the one I was now in. Another time, another place, another country, family and personality I embodied.

"What does it all mean?" I asked..... and as I asked, I remembered something..... I remembered that when I was travelling in England I had taken a wrong bus and ended up at Westminster Abbey. I had to post a letter and was told there was a post office in the Abbey. I went in and saw on the ground, a silver, memorial plaque which was in memory of Catherine. I had cried and cried at the sight of it, with no logical explanation, for over half an hour, deep gut wrenching tears. I had seen the Tower of London from a distance and felt a welling of tears within me, a lump in my throat, and had wondered why. I knew this had some relation to what was happening now. I felt it within. I had memory of it in this life even though it had been unconscious and I did not understand it then, I felt it and I understood it now. I closed my eyes once more.

The memory of my father was so clear; the tiered, lace dress shirt, the head held high. He had a wit and humour that I loved and his intelligence seemed beyond that of many. Yet never at any time did he sit in arrogance or condescension. He looked for the God in people and recognised the absence of God in others. He was no fool.

I had learned a great deal from him and were it not for societal pressures I never would have married as I felt married to him, even though he was my father. He was the one for whom I lived. Some thought our relationship was unhealthy, but it was simply love, a deep love between father and daughter. I admired him and aspired to be as he was, as did many. I was his favourite. He also spoke highly of me and commended my efforts, pushing me to greater heights in my achievements. With him behind me life had meaning and purpose. Now he was gone. The meaning and purpose seemed to go also.

My husband, William, had a task in getting my attention. He was supportive enough but I really did not care for him a great deal. Even though we had children together, it seemed more the nanny's task to look after them than mine. We were to move from here, this house where we had shared so much time; time when we had looked forward to the King's visits, for he was my father's friend. I remembered those times with fond memory and I had great difficulty understanding how the King could ask for his beheadal. When I had taken the head from the pike I had felt deep pain within me, but I did not let it show. I summoned all the courage I could muster to achieve that task. In claiming his head I was demanding that his integrity be recognised. Many thought I had gone mad; a volatile, imbalanced woman, overwhelmed by grief. They felt pity for me. The anger I felt within was great. I did not need pity. Nothing could bring that love back. With the loss of the physical presence of my father I closed my heart to many in the court. I felt I could take no more, but more were taken, more heads guillotined and my heart closed even more tightly. The woman I was, passionate, enthusiastic, with zest and love for life and all it represented, had died. I became instead the embodiment of anger and bitterness, not allowing my grief to be seen by anyone, not even felt by myself.

It was not until this lifetime when I saw the tower of London and the plaque in memory of Catherine that grief was again triggered. It had been held within for centuries and only now, having made the decision to open my heart again, could it be released.

It was time to leave, the chests were packed and the carriage came to get us. Anne and Elizabeth were to arrive that afternoon. The house needed to be free for them to enter. The King had ordered that the departure take place by the eleventh hour. I felt no malice that I had to leave the house for it acted like a skewer to my heart, needling the pain. I could no longer stand the memories, the visions, for I saw him standing everywhere and I heard him speak to me even though he was gone. I could take him with me in my heart and I felt him there until the day I died ...... I had found it difficult to live with myself. I knew William was capable of looking after the children. I began to eat very little. I lost the will to live and some short time after my father's death, I died. Ironically, I felt my death a death of principle, unfortunately based on wrong motive. There seemed little I could do about it as nothing in life seemed to touch me anymore. Perhaps they were right, perhaps I was mad in those later stages. I had certainly got beyond the point of reaching out to anyone and my brave front ensured that no-one would reach in to me. It wasn't until after that lifetime, when again I returned to soul, that I understood he had not been deserted by the God of whom he so often spoke. In the Light of soul I could feel the Love of God and his at-one-ness with that love. He had been taken for Higher purpose, I knew, and the anger I had in the personality as Margaret, dissipated.

When I once again connected with soul I could see that the lesson for me to understand was what my father had always tried to convey: it is God's law that must be adhered to and not man's law, God's sense of timing, God's plan and not man's. I began to understand that I did not always have to understand. I could see too that that is sometimes difficult when one is in physical incarnation and one feels the grief of personality.

I asked within me, "How does it relate to me now? Why am I being shown this?" The answer came with a force and a knowing that cut straight through any fear I had.

"You are frightened to love now through fear of loss, through fear of betrayal. You must recognise the karma involved and not blame anyone for the events that occurred. You must be aware that through your loss you learned the depth of your love. In this life, remember the depth of your love and you will find that loss is not necessary. Even when loss occurs you will know that it is only physical, for the love has remained with you for all the people involved. Love is eternal. There should be no attachment to form life. Let love flow. Do not be frightened of it this time for there is no loss. Love grows and develops over centuries and aeons of time. It is never lost. It is all that is."

It all made sense. More sense than anything I had felt for some time. It began a series of events, learnings and understandings about my life this time and lifetimes gone which carried within them a similar thread, a similar pattern. Every time I looked I seemed to find another incidence of the fear of loss and betrayal.

*..... I stood in uniform and stared at the tower that held her captive. I wanted so much to communicate and let her know she had not been deserted. I felt her love, her passion, her dedication to Christ, to Archangel Michael. * My love for her had developed through the day to day actions of carrying out set tasks that I*

carried out unquestioningly. Anything I would do for I knew the purity of her heart, the commitment and dedication to the cause of allowing the spirit to manifest on earth, the spirit of the Divine. I found it difficult as I stood watching the tower everyday. I kept expecting that she would be freed, but she was not. I began to feel an incredible frustration within. I was unable to make physical contact. She was to burn. I was unable to do anything about it. I kept thinking that the Christ would save her. I watched her burn. I became angry at Christ, angry at Archangel Michael. I believed that God had deserted her. I was concerned that she would feel deserted. I felt enormous frustration and anger within me at losing her.

As she burned I felt loss and betrayal. Both of these energies were very strong within me. I felt overwhelmed by grief and quickly suppressed this grief that I felt so painful to feel. It was easier to blame God, to cry out "traitor." In doing that I did not have to face the deep bottomless pit of pain within me. An enormous frustration rose up from inside. I couldn't bear to be with myself. It was a pain that was strange and unfamiliar. It took over my whole being. I found I could not control the grief. It leapt up at every opportunity and I attached myself tightly to the blame, in the hope that I could get some control back in my life. The frustration was further accentuated by the events that followed, for I, and others who followed her, were also to burn. It was only a matter of time. I, too, was held captive. The grief became many-fold: the grief for those around me who were dying, for the loss of my own life, and for the loss of the true knowledge of spirit that was being made extinct through our death. At least this was how I saw it. The anger I had towards Christ increased. Yet at the same time I felt the joy at being able to serve Him in this way. There was much bloodshed, much suffering undergone in this period of history, and I felt the pain that humanity had not perceived the Truth to be worthy of embrace and acknowledgment.

She did not feel deserted. In time I came to understand that she had instead been taken for higher purpose. I did not understand nor was I meant to understand the workings of Maitreya.* When I could finally see the wrongness of my thinking, I began to understand much. It took several lifetimes for the pain was so great, the love so deep and the loss, in my mind, so enormous. The personality could not cope with the sudden severance. I closed my heart through fear of pain, through fear of having to face loss of love so great again. She was an example of great courage and faith, never giving up, never deserting, nor feeling desertion; an inspiration to be sure. She had something I could only aim for, absolute faith in the Divine.

Many times I saw myself frightened to open my heart, frightened to love.

.....I brushed her hair and placed the brush upon the dresser. There were pink roses on the back of the brush. I stared at them. I had become familiar with everything in the room. I had been in the same physical proximity for a long time now, waiting on her. I was seething inside, deciding I did not like her. I joked and played outwardly so that this insidious feeling within me could not be seen. I felt enormous guilt for she was the Queen and I the maid, the lady in waiting. Marion, I was called. My existence became frightful to me as the guilt grew and the disdain for her words and her being also grew. I began to feel as though I were in a pressure cooker. So close in proximity, so little life of my own, I tended her every whim. I began to fantasise and scheme about escape. I felt totally hemmed in, trapped. When I would meet with the other maids I would gossip to pass the time. It seemed the only way I could find joy and that added to the guilt. The solution came, a flash in the mind. I would do it.

I wrote a letter and addressed it to myself. I paid one of the servants to go out of town and post it for me so that it would arrive and I could pretend I didn't know its contents. I was brushing her hair when it came. I opened it as she beckoned me to do so. I looked confused and alarmed.

"It's my mother'" I said. "She's dying. I must go to her."
"Yes, of course." she said.

I made plans to leave the court, I scurried off looking down. I could not look her in the eyes anymore. My paranoia had taken me over, my fear and hatred had filled me. There was no compassion nor mercy left in me. No love, just fear. I felt guilt that followed me as I left. The freedom that I thought I would find escaped me. Instead the guilt grew heavier, the burden greater. I did not know where I was going to or what I would do. I found refuge in an old house amongst the villagers. I changed my clothes to poor people's clothes. I took off the velvet garments, the lace and the riches. I cut off my hair and applied for jobs cleaning, sweeping the streets, selling mussels, anything I could find. I worked and worked, trying to take my mind off what I had done. I had no sense of self worth left, and no sense of loyalty to the Queen. I buried myself in my pain, fear and guilt, until, finally, I died.

I had closed my heart in that lifetime because of the fear of being close to anyone, the fear of losing love again. With a closed heart I could not open and be in such close proximity with another. It was too much for me to bear. It constantly challenged the closed door of my heart. I had much to learn about respect and loyalty; respecting others' privacy, respecting others and myself, and opening myself to love. It seemed I had completely closed down to the Christ energy. I did not feel worthy of life and was driven to death through guilt.

I needed to understand that guilt is used by those not of love to destroy any element of love or life force, that is positive. There was no fun in the life I saw. No life or lightness, just darkness and pain. I returned searching, in lives to come, for more meaning, for ways to move out of that death trap of guilt and of low and despicable self esteem, that led me in that life to project it so totally on to another human being as I had done to the Queen.

I was beginning to understand and know even more deeply the truth of what was revealed to me during the death experience I had in hospital. I was discovering the voice of God within me. I did need to learn to trust.

I needed to learn to trust myself, others and God. The voice came in many forms. It confronted and questioned every attitude, value and belief about God and God's existence, about the world and how it was. There was something about this voice within me, this knowing, that I felt I had to trust at every turn. There were other voices I had to be aware of also. I began to learn the need for discrimination.

No longer could I seek God through external circumstance, because I knew otherwise. God was in me. Everything that was in me that was not of God had to be let go of in order that I might find God within. It seemed that no matter what I thought, how I perceived the world with all its paradoxes and differences, everything made sense in a greater Plan, beyond my level of comprehension. All I could really do was let go and let God.

Chapter 10

THE WAY OF THE HEART

December 31st, 1986 Glenormiston

Many events had led to my being there, on this special night.
It was New Year's Eve. I had been travelling overseas some
months earlier, feeling as if I would never return to Australia. I
was travelling with a different perspective from my first journey.
Still, the journey was somewhat escapist in nature. I had begun
to accumulate many goods. My pack was quite heavy from the
load of unnecessary attachments I had made. I had written poems,
painted paintings, taken pictures and accumulated many gifts from
those I had met along the way. I was beginning to feel dissatisfied
with the perennial change of people, places and things in my life.

I was robbed. The shock was enormous, everything taken. Yet the
initial thought was relief at not having to carry the pack any more.
I had to wire home for money. To pay it back I had to return to
work in Australia. Some days after arriving home the second time,
I saw the brochure. There was to be a Retreat in Glenormiston, a
twelve day sojourn. Something inside me knew I had to go. I had
no money but I rang anyway and asked if I could come - trusting
that I would be able to pay later. The lady on the other end of the
phone was very open to me, her voice bright and chirpy. She told
me she would ring back and let me know, and she did.

Many were gathered that evening. We had been in retreat for some
days already and I had felt many changes occur within me. There
was something more immediate and real in the way these people

viewed the world. There were people there from other countries, and on this night Ananda Tara Shan* was to lead the service.

It began much the same as others I had attended, and though anticipation was high, I was not aware of the power and light that would come that evening. The service had begun. Many people were present in coloured vestments. The huge hall was filled, everybody creating a circle to witness the event. Ananda began to channel, and then it came. A huge golden sun descended and radiated forth. It was as if the Sun itself was coming down from its position in the sky. With it came a beautiful feeling of warmth and an enormous Light. It sent waves of tingling throughout my whole being. So gentle, I'd never felt anything like it before. As my eyes were closed I could see tinges of a most beautiful pink, along with the gold. The Sun was moving throughout my whole body until I was one with it. I felt my heart expand. My heart became tangible. Every cell was alive and vibrating with this Sun. The energy was finer and lighter than anything I had felt before. It merged with everything, even the Earth itself. All around me were vibrating in this new Light. Everyone else's hearts touched, tears flowing. Maitreya had come.

It began to make sense within me. A new path of development was being created. I was now beginning to see it. It was the Way of the Heart.

September 29, 1987 Melbourne

It was St. Michael's day. We had been preparing for the ceremony for some time. I was spending more and more time amongst the spiritual group run by Ananda Tara Shan. I felt as though I were among family. Being there gave expression to the spiritual aspects of myself that I had discovered. I had decided from a very deep place within me that it was time for me to enter into the spirit world in earnest, to take conscious decision to take part in what I could see was a way of helping the earth and mankind, to be a part of a responsible order and take my place, once again, amongst beings of light. It was a choice I had deliberated over. It had taken some years for me to work through the trappings of my personality in order to be aligned with this choice. The time had come.

There was a very strong air of festivity. The celebration was to be held in a huge hall in Melbourne. Spiritual people from many places came to be part of this ceremony. It was for me a time when I was entering into the Order. The night came. There was an air of anticipation. People were taking their places in their seats. Guests were entering with a sense of awe at the grandness of the event. Those in the ceremony were clothed in an array of various, brightly coloured vestments. There was silence as the crowd came to a hush. The music began. I was sitting in a purple vestment in the wings. As I sat there I could feel a very deep centering taking place within me. Within a very short time I could feel the presence of a huge angel behind me. It felt as though it were attaching itself to me. There was something very calming about it. I could feel the wings of this enormous being flapping. My own arms took the shape of the wings. I felt very at One with it. I felt that the flight of spirit had begun.

Ananda called me up. I stood in front of her. As I walked towards her and stood before her it was as if a huge movie screen opened up before me. I was shown a heart with three daggers in it. She began to sing and I felt a wind of beautiful energy rushing through my whole being. I became, then, part of the movie I had seen. The heart was mine and the daggers were piercing it. It felt almost physical. One by one I pulled the daggers from my heart and threw them aside. It seemed to take some effort, with each one I grappled. I knew they were daggers I had placed in my own heart, through fear, guilt and feelings of low self worth. One by one I pulled them out. They had been marring the connection to my own heart. More and more Light came down upon me with such force that I felt impelled to go with it. A force-field of energy was drawing me in. I went up a tunnel where I came to a doorway. Ananda was that doorway. The door opened. There was a path, a golden path that lead to a pink heart. The path was windy, clear and pure. The light was full of colour, yet really fine, like a mist. Along the side of the path it was green. Along it were red and white roses, red at the entrance, becoming white as the path moved along. I knew I was to walk this path. As I entered I was given a white rose. I could see the most beautiful heart ahead, huge and pink, the most intense, vibrant pink I had ever seen. I felt it would totally envelop me. Within it was all the life there is. It was the Way of the Heart before me. I began to walk.

In choosing to let go of the daggers I had been using to abuse my own spirit, my own self, I was able to connect with the wisdom and love of this path.

The shift in consciousness had come. Now I could begin my work in the west in earnest. I knew that though the road was not an easy one, the decision had been made, the daggers left behind. The path was full of Light. I knew that on it many gifts would be bestowed. It was my responsibility to keep walking on that path. I could not go back now. Nor did I want to. I had come too far.

The ceremony continued. There was much joy and festivity that evening. People sharing, open hearted. People alive in consciousness, connecting with one another at levels higher than normal in vibration.

That evening I went home. I cried deep, deep tears, deeper than I can ever remember crying within me. Something had cracked.

I felt strong pain in my heart and I knew that the deep wounds within it were beginning to heal. I knew that I had to jump into the most wounded part of my being without fear in order to find this healing. I knew that the heart of Christ was around me now. I had been lifted into that heart, the heart of Maitreya, the Lord of Love. My life would be different now. The tears were for the past I was leaving behind.

It seemed there was an electrical storm. It came quickly. Many coloured vestments lined the walls, people ready for the event. Invocations were made. The service began. Ananda began to channel through energy and words, and then it hit me like a bolt of lightning from the sky. She pointed two fingers, and as she did, the lightning spread throughout the room. I, and several others fell to the floor lying horizontal. All those in vestments were told to lie down. I felt as though someone had pointed a fire-hose, full-blast down my spine. I could feel the energy surging through all my chakras vivifying them. Through the crown, up from the base chakra, up and down, round and round the energy swirled. I knew the chakras were spiritual centres within the body. I had never felt them as clearly as this. Each one felt like a trap door opening, and I was aware as the energy hit each one that a tremendous explosion was taking place within me. Finally my focus was taken to my heart. From here the energy seemed to expand and I felt my heart in a way I had never felt it, glowing and warm and tingling all over. I could feel spiritual ecstasy. The music stopped, the channelling stopped and I found myself horizontal on the floor, a little amazed that I had lain there in the first place. I got to my feet aware that something had happened. An energy and light of great magnitude had descended through Ananda and somehow become a part of all those present.

As people left the service that night, it took them longer to start speaking than usual. Each trying to fathom the depth of this new reality within, knowing that the heart had been touched in a way not before known. It triggered within me the memory of Avalon....

She wielded great power. Her name was Morgaine, and it was she who helped to train the priestesses of the order. I would see her often

*walking with the Merlin. She had the key to the Ancient Mysteries.
I was a priestess taken by the light; devoted and pious. I admired
her and I was frightened of her. For she seemed to know so much
and mirror so much of me. Whenever there was anything I needed
to learn, it would come to me through her presence. Thoughtforms
of different kinds of varying strengths were her method of teaching.
Whether she was aware or not, she was used as a vehicle for the
teachings I needed, and many others around me also. On other
levels, she was busy working for the earth, bringing forth the light
of Archangel Michael. Making sure that spirit could stay manifest
in a world where humanity's dogmas were beginning to suppress it.
She walked along in her flowing gowns; everybody noticed. For she
had a strength and a being that was not common in that time for
a woman. A character beyond reproach, functioning as it needed
to function to bring down light, and not more. Her way of being
was very confonting for society at that time, for she walked in
Truth, in God's law and not in alignment with man's. She was
not without foibles, part of her own process, and this caused her
much suffering. Many were frightened of her like I was, because
she had the capacity to mirror the darkness within all in order that
it might be recognised and dealt with.*

*There came a time in that life when her power had to be exposed.
Structures were beginning to descend in humanity's religions that
were not allowing the flow of spirit to come forth. The Light of the
Holy Grail needed to be felt within the hearts of all to remind us of
our spiritual nature. At this time many were using religious dogma
as a means to deny Spirit, as a political ploy to gain material
possessions and land, to build up a hierarchy based on power,
and not love nor light, not spiritual in any way. Many had taken
to gossiping about her, putting her in such a negative light that
it made it difficult for her truth to be revealed. The dogmatic
structures were taking the form of restrictive energies suppressing*

Light and they needed to be destroyed in order that the Light of Michael, that the Will of God, could once again come through.

It was King Arthur's birthday, and people had come from everywhere. Knights and ladies from all over England were in attendance. It seemed everyone was present. All the people who considered themselves to be the holders of the power; Dukes and Duchesses, coming together for the glamour of the event, rather than the joy of seeing one another. Morgaine wore red that day and walked as if there were a crown upon her head. Eyes turned as she walked by, unable to look elsewhere, for her energy was like a magnet. There was something about her that day which could not go unnoticed. She went to Arthur and sat down. He seemed to have lost some of his sensitivity to her cause and yet was obviously attracted by her presence that day. He sat with her for some time which was something he had been avoiding, as it reminded him of his own dedication to the light of the goddess which was still present deep within. The minstrels were playing, the feast was magnificent. As ladies and knights entered they were introduced and led to their seats. Time came for the festivities to come into their fullness. The plays were presented by the players, who did their best to please the King. I had followed her this day from the isle of Avalon. I and several others had felt to support her, though we knew not what in. It was clear there was work to be done, so we were dressed in street clothes of colours and shapes unlike those we were used to on the isle. It was quite a day. The air was thick with festivity, and it was clear that there had built up within that community, a degree of resentment towards her. It was obvious that there was fear of her Light, the Light of the Goddess, of the Mother. As I followed in the wings, I had glimpses of this energy through the trail she left behind. Something had to be done to make a shift, to change this energy and break through the dogmas and narrow structures constricting spirit through people's negative thought. It was on this *night that Morgaine revealed herself. The bard was playing angelic music of the harp, and she rose for all to see, sending the Light of Archangel Michael like thunder into the evening. People could not ignore her power for it thundered through all their narrow-minded, limited thoughts. Those with eyes to see, ears to hear and hearts to feel, felt the Presence of the Mother Christ. She wore the crown of the Diamond Light of Tara the White. It could not be denied. The Spirit of the Mother lives on.*

Deep within me my heart had been touched on this New Year's Eve night. It had touched a part of me that lives forever, and I could see that Avalon lives still. Perhaps a new Light but still with the essence of love as its centre. The Ancient Mysteries are revealed to those who open, and are prepared to listen with their hearts. Understandings were coming. Glimpses of insight arose within me, and I felt tiny in comparison to the ever-living Presence of the Mother Light. Its depth was unfathomable, its loving power nourishing, and within it was the chance of complete surrender. The perennial Heart Light appeared before me and began to awaken the memory within.

Chapter 11

SEEDS OF ACCEPTANCE

The breathlessness began to overtake me once more. It was the middle of the night when it began, as it always did, making it evident to me that it existed deeply within the realms of my unconsciousness. I would wake in fear, not able to take in life. This morning it was about 4.30 a.m. I woke alone in my bedroom surrounded by the walls and an almost clinical feeling. My lungs had totally seized and breath was not coming in or out. I had been living in this house for some time and was used to going with this feeling in the early hours of the morning until it resolved itself. That usually involved taking various sorts of drugs, that I had got from the doctor, until the asthma passed, sitting with my fear of death and the unknowable for the time it took for the drugs to take effect. I even had a gas mask, or a ventilator, which I could use to help me get air into my lungs. This particular morning nothing seemed to work. Some three hours of struggle had gone by and I heard footsteps as other household members began to get up and begin their daily activities. I was fortunate that the people I lived with were conscious of metaphysical realities. When they heard my struggle they came to help. It was the first time I had actually decided to confront this fear whilst I was in it. I had done healings and therapy sessions about this fear and found various understandings and insights that had helped me a great deal. This time however I could confront it directly for it was there.

I closed my eyes and went with the process. I created an image to represent my fear. An image came forward; it was a set of hands attached to white arms that had upon them, yellow gloves. They were squeezing my bronchials tightly. I asked them what they were doing.

"We're here because you empowered us to be here." They said. "We squeeze your breath out of you every time you begin to feel pleasure and contentment in life."

"Why? " I asked.

"Because you told us to. You do not feel worthy of happiness." I was somewhat surprised but it made sense. Then within the process I began to become one with this set of hands and I looked back at myself through their eyes. What I saw was a lump of skin with a round belly, legs and arms knotted, and a sallow face. It was quite a sight. The legs were draped in a yogi position. The general sense of an old yogi inhabiting an undernourished body was the essence of what I saw. I asked if there was anything that I, as these hands, wanted to say to Cheryl. I felt so grateful for the opportunity to speak to her.

"There is great imbalance between the nourishment you give yourself on the physical level and the energy you put to spiritual practices. You need to allow the spiritual energies with which you meditate to come within your being. They cannot get in, they just flow all around you because you do not love yourself. You must learn to love your body, to treat it as a Temple through which the spiritual energies can come through. There is great neglect here. Further to this you make us punish you by making us squeeze your bronchials whenever there is any sense of pleasure within your life. You really don't feel worthy of life and that is why you do not breathe in the air because you feel unworthy of life itself."

The realisation of this entered my being and the image changed to a scene which could only be described as horrific. It was very much like what I had seen on television in "The World at War" series. The word Auschwitz came into my consciousness. I could see many naked bodies, many people full of fear, and I was one of them. We *were naked and we were to take showers when it began, hundreds of us. The children had been taken much earlier. Many others had already been killed in the firing lines or tortured. I had been kept longer as I was a pretty one. The despair I felt was enormous. The deaths already witnessed, the grief already being felt. My time had come. The memory of that time was being felt from deep within me.*

The gas began to enter. Body upon body fell to the ground, choking, so many bodies, the touch of flesh, the oppression of the gas. A few moments of contemplation before the death was enough time to decide that God had rejected the Jewish race; to blame God and find that I was not worthy of life for God had decided to kill me. Even though it was not the truth, it was what I had decided. The hands reappeared.

"You see," they said, "You decided a long time ago that you were not worthy of life. You need to change that decision if you are to accept life in this lifetime, for it thwarts you now. On days when the sky is grey, where the pollution is strong, it activates within you a memory, and within that memory a decision, that you are not worth it after all. Your body responds by closing down. It will take time to desensitise yourself from this process, from this memory. There are many levels upon which you must work to do this, for it is multi causal and effects you on all levels; physical, emotional, mental and spiritual. You can try homoeopathy, it is a sacred science. You must work physiologically and spiritually and change the thoughts of mind. It will take time but at least now you are aware of part of the cause, part of the wrong thoughts that contribute to your part of the karma and the state of disease. Imagine yourself on those days when the sky is going grey. Visualise instead pink light, breathing it in with joy, saying to yourself, "There is plenty of air for me. I deserve life for I am life. I am the

Resurrection and the life." I knew that I was commencing a whole new way of seeing my disease, a whole new way of approaching life.

These were the seeds that I was given and they came as a result of my prayers for help, for guidance, for understanding. They were, at this time seeds and they would grow into new thoughts, new life. From them in time I would find leaves of understanding and healing. For my part I had to water them and give them space to grow within my body, my mind, my spirit. I could do this by remaining open and by being aware that I know nothing. In that way I could learn Everything.

Chapter 12

INTEGRITY

I began to see Asthma in a new light.

It is all in the way you see it, the way you perceive it.

The image came this time clearly, the plastic mask, part of the Asthma ventilator. Immediately upon seeing it I felt ill, a strong physical reaction, seeing it as meaning rejection from God.

It had an oppressive energy. A force from which I wanted to move away. I spoke to it.

"I feel that you are trying to force me into powerlessness, into being the victim. I don't think you should have that power any more."

"But in this lifetime I help you." it replied.

I became aware of the energy of safety and relief that I got from the mask in this lifetime and felt confused. Two aspects present at the same time, a killing force and a life force. It answered.

"I am the same, it is the way in which you see me, the way you perceive me. I can be anything you make me into. You decide what I am; the power you give to me or the power that you don't give to me."

I remembered the hands and the power I had given them and I began to understand further.

"Why am I confronted by you in this lifetime?" I asked.

"You haven't always been, but now you are more relaxed and less fearful of life. You have come to a state where you don't feel rejected by God but are beginning to accept God."

"Is there a way I can overcome the need to use you, and be me."

"Be the power you have given to me; make the decision to live, to breathe, to have flow in life. Be the life force." It replied. I could feel myself becoming that life force.

Again the scene of many Jewish people screaming in fear, enclosed by big cement walls returned and I was seeing it this time through new eyes. The mask said.

"They don't see that they have the ability to control the life force. There is a very suppressive energy there, a total contrast to when one takes one's true power and is the decision to live, to be one with the life force. Oppression is only oppression when one person gives the power away. A victim is only a victim when another takes the power. It takes two."

I could see again when I was in Sri Lanka, the man raping me. I decided for the first time I would not be oppressed. I would not be the victim and I acknowledged in fighting for that time that God didn't want me to be one either. In taking integrity by the hand I could stop blaming God for the way I have seen things in my past. I could see more now, that it is only in my own perception that I have been the victim. It hasn't been the truth.

I feel that I could look down on all the incidents in this life and other lives that I have seen myself as the victim and change them now in my Consciousness.

The mask continued, "The gas in the death chambers represents the horrible power which the masses created. Nothing has that power unless we give into it. It is all up to us. We have but to recognise that we have strength within us and there is a united power that we can tap into. In choosing to unite with this strength we can eradicate victim and oppressor consciousness. We can find the power to do that in love, love that goes beyond our understanding of love at this time. It has to do with complete unselfishness, service and unity, totally turning ourselves outwards, all our cells living for everyone else. It is a new way of serving the world that is without martyrdom and without self concern. It is a world concern through which man will really come to understand love. People have to stop thinking that everything which happens to them has great consequence. When we get concerned with ourselves we take up energies that could be otherwise used to liberate the world. Our freedom will come when we look beyond ourselves. We go within to find God and in order to reach universal knowing we must bring that inner God outwards and manifest it in our daily lives."

I looked at the mask and it had lost its power. It looked like a piece of plastic and I felt that on a cellular level, a change had taken place.

Chapter 13

JUSTICE

I was dressed in white, a man of the cloth. The ornate headdress and cross of colour upon the vestment gave me a sense of superiority. I was a cardinal. I did not feel at all holy. Instead I felt full of contempt for mankind, full of hate, full of empty power. Huge wooden doors opened before me and I went through. I could see as I looked down from the balcony upon which I now stood a large crowd of Spanish looking people. They were in a state of unrest, angry, yelling words of abuse in my direction. These people were in a state of revolt. I looked upon them with utter detestation, seeing them as nothing more than scum deserving to be killed. I walked back into the vestry and sat down at a large wooden desk. I took the quill in hand and began to sign the orders that would bring about the end of the lives of many who were now outside yelling their grievances. It felt good. I felt cold, manipulative and calculating, thriving on power for power's sake. I felt they deserved to be killed. There was not an ounce of compassion within me.

It was hard for me to stay with this image and these feelings within me. Here I was, the supposedly good natured, loving Cheryl, seeing a part of myself that was far from that. It was hard for me to believe but everything else that had been shown made sense and felt right so I stayed with it a little longer. I had been quite willing to attribute these motives of power and callousness in my perceptions and judgements of others. Never before had I found this nature so prominently aspected in my own being. Here it was, large as life, fully embodied in this grotesque, male appearance before me. I began to know without doubt that it was a part of me. It was showing itself for redemption. In meeting it I was forced to reconsider my judgements of others and myself. I could see that it was not for me to judge or criticise or blame others, for I have my own shadow, my own darkness. I am not always an angel.

As I watched I felt within me a tendency to take on full guilt for this aspect of my past. I began to realise also, that for redemption to occur, I needed to let go of that guilt, to drop my judgements of others and forgive myself for my own past. It had come to me now to teach me about love. I began to see that the lifetimes I had had as victim were really quite karmic. There was a sense of relief with this as I could let it go. A cosmic balancing was evident. I felt the need to bring in a new state of awareness; that of equality and responsibility for the choices and actions I take in life. The repercussions of my actions in that lifetime were evident in those that followed. Here was the test; to recognise that which is done, forgive and move on. I had to learn to let go of guilt and see that it perpetuated a negative condition which kept me trapped in the illusion that I was bad, that I didn't deserve life.

The cardinal spoke to me.

"You have come a long way since me. You have now developed within your heart a true compassion and love of life. You need not hold yourself back anymore, through fear of being rejected by me or through guilt for what I have done. Payment has been made. Justice has been done. Redemption will occur when you realise this. Allow yourself to align with soul and make new choices based on this releasing of the past. You are in essence a being of free will now and are asked to exercise that free will at every point, every direction in your life now. It is a moment by moment decision that determines the direction of your spiritual evolution. When you come to understand this, judgement of self and others drops away. You will realise that it is the Christ within which judges

only. Guilt is one thing, conscience another. With clear conscience, that comes from clear motive and purity of heart, you can walk ahead in your life, leaving behind all that has held you back. All you need is the simple recognition that man decides. Light or dark, man decides.

I could feel a great sense of responsibility with these words and a huge amount of relief. It was as if the weight of the past lifted, the weight of guilt that I had created and been servant to. I could see that my power came from my heart, through my compassion and my love. In choosing to radiate that power life moves to a new place where one can be in alignment with the Divine and all things become possible.

Chapter 14

BEYOND INTELLECT

It was the late nineteenth century. I was a theosophist. I could feel the thirst for spirit within me as I read and read all the theosophical teachings I could get my hands on. I was trying desperately to find spirit in intellect, thinking I would find the answer in books. I left England and went to America hoping to find that spirit amongst the teachings of my contemporaries. I was searching for a sense of brother and sisterhood. I talked and talked, read and read, yearning within for contact with the Divine. I had spent many years in this search and at the end of many long nights of discussion would go home and write up my thoughts, my philosophies. There were times when I was asked to speak in various countries and I dutifully met the task required.

I spent much of the lifetime alone, unmarried, burning the candle late at night in my room full of books and thought. One night in spirit, Madame Blavatsky spoke to me. Her presence was huge and her words clear,

"I will always be with you in spirit. The door is always open to one with an open heart."

I could feel her essence permeate my being. I could feel oneness with the Divine. Her image was there larger than life and I could feel the energy of truth within, all encompassing, all embracing. I could collapse in that embrace readily. It lifted me out of confusion, out of my intellect, which had been battling to find truth. In her Presence I could feel truth in every cell of my body. I knew she spoke it. I no longer had to linger in the trappings of the lower mind for I came to know and sense what was higher mind, Divine mind. Within me I felt an alignment take place, a bonding that was eternal and infinite. The confusion and questions, deliberations of thought, discussions and intellectuality I had previously embarked upon seemed meaningless in contrast. I could feel the energy of Mother Christ and felt great joy within my soul. At last I had opened my heart to the Christ, the heart energy. It filled the room and I pulsed with it. I knew as she spoke that I would do anything to bring that light and love to earth.

Chapter 15

THE HEALING TREE

I began to think that if we learn through our disease, then maybe if I prayed hard enough, I could learn another way. Not through asthma, although that taught me a lot, but a way that was easier for me to deal with, not so debilitating in my day to day world. Soon after I made this prayer I got a strong toothache and although I didn't immediately connect the two, I discovered in time there was indeed connection. There was something my tooth wanted to say to me, so I decided to look at it.

An image came forward of my tooth, the gum was very red, the tooth very white, the roots very deep. It was the six year old molar. I asked the tooth what it wanted to tell me or show me. The vision came. I was taken back to a time when I was a child, very small in the play pen and I could feel a real sense of safety in this play pen, grateful that I could be in this space and not further out in the world I saw beyond the bars. I stayed in the comfortable space for a short time and really let myself feel it. It felt beautiful. I could also feel a sense of curiosity about what lay outside the bars.

The scene changed and I was six years old. By this stage I was at the tennis courts with my mother. It was a happy phase in her life. She was quite self actualised, content with her friends and lifestyle. She was playing tennis, an 'A' Grade pennant player, dressed in her whites. It was a sunny day. I could hear the impact of the tennis ball hitting the racquet and the sounds of the umpire calling "Net!", "Fault!" and "Love!" The sounds were deep and rich and I could sense the fullness of concentration the adults had upon the game. I watched for some time. It seemed important this game,

89

every hit counted, every hit mattered. There were smiles enough once the game had ended, a generally good feeling as the ladies came off the court. Thermoses of tea and an array of various cakes were presented. Mum had made lemon meringue pie which was my favourite. It was all I could do to stop myself sneaking some before we left home. Mum had a sense of knowing where she was in the world and how to go about being in the world. I felt safe with her. She loved life and all with which she was presented. Over in a corner I could see a baby in a play pen. I went over to it whilst the women were chatting. As I held the bars and stood before it I watched it chew upon a crust that its mother had given it. I could sense the feeling of dependency and safety it had. Standing there I could feel myself in dilemma. I was six years old, too young to be as dependent as the child in the play pen and not old enough to be as confident and assured as my mother. I began to wonder why I was seeing this image and I began not to like the feeling of confusion I felt so I asked the tooth. I was aware that I really didn't want to be with my mother at this place although I was happy that she was happy. I could not be like the child in the play pen. I could not be like my mother. There was nowhere for me to be, no place for me and this was the essence of my confusion. The tooth explained,

"You have choice now. The baby is completely dependent on others. The mother is fully active and the girl is hesitating between the two. The mother is happy, the baby is happy, but the girl is torn by indecision. You are thwarted by indecision."
"Indecision about what? " I asked.
"About being here. Make full commitment to being alive, there is no need to fear it."

I could sense that I wanted to be like my mother. The tooth told me I could do it and let myself love life to the fullest.

90

"Be open in your relationship, fully. Everything is there to have a full life. All you have to do is have it. To have it all, all that you have to do is to decide to have it. Your parents' ways of doing things do not have to be yours anymore. You have grown up."

"Why does my tooth hurt?" I asked.

"It has to do with choosing the right structure. You see the little girl in you feels as though she never gets what she wants. You can help her grow and change that. When children teethe, they change from having the world look after them to accepting the world as different and becoming more independent in it. As you are now becoming adult in a real sense, you also have to move in your perceptions of the world and take responsibility, initiative and action. Do not be frightened to move forward in it. There is not the same need to ask for permission. When you were young, you needed the boundaries, the limits, around you like the child in the play pen. They are changing. For you are becoming self actualised in life."

In my consciousness I was very aware of the definition of the roots, the strength of the tooth and the contrast between the tooth and the gums.

" Your life is quite well defined, if you choose to see it and the roots run deep, the foundation is strong. It has strength. Open to this strength. You have pain because of moving beyond the play pen and your fear is not being able to find a space for yourself in life. Many have this fear. It takes decision and will. You must make this. It has to come from you, then the universe can empower you in it. The first decision is to decide to live and love, the rest takes care of itself, you will see."

I thought about what I had been told and wondered how I could help the girl within me grow up. I had found it difficult to contain her, for at times she got very angry. For even though I was an adult I could feel her within me, an explosion of childish emotion with no basis in rationality. She would appear when I would least expect her to and create havoc in my life. She seemed selfish and stubborn and I had taken to doing things that she wanted as it seemed to be the only way to deal with her.

"How can I help her grow?" I asked.

"Just recognise her and don't be controlled by her. She demands much and doesn't want things to change. Watch out for her, you will see her more clearly now that I have pointed her out, speak to her and comfort her but do not let her take control. She will not be able to manipulate you in the way that she has done for she has been exposed like the nerve of the tooth. It will not take long to heal, it will just take awareness, love and patience and these qualities are being developed within you."

"It takes time to change one's perceptions of the world, especially when one keeps anticipating failure, or the manifestation of one's fears and doubts. To look at the world from a positive viewpoint, to see that life might not be as bad as we think it is, or as bad as we have painted our past, all this takes time. Be patient with yourself. There are parts of you that need to be healed in order that you may become whole. These parts are showing themselves to you now. Trust this part of your process, for it will lead to wholeness, into a full and loving life. Go to the dentist, you will need that help on the physical level."

I was happy for that advice and I went to the dentist. I discovered that it was not my six year old molar that was the problem but the eight year old.

"I don't understand it," I said to the dentist," are you sure it's not my six year old molar?"

"Sometimes pain transfers, to another tooth. When the pain gets too much for us to bear we transfer it to another tooth and feel it there. The tooth is split completely, down the middle."

He dressed the nerve, filled it and I went home. When the injection wore off and the pain returned I was aware from our conversation that I needed to look more deeply, there was something more I needed to see, some deep pain of which I needed to let go.

I closed my eyes and went within. From a very deep place I asked to be able to see, understand and release the pain that I needed to release. A scene presented itself to me from my childhood. I could see my father. He was in a psychiatric hospital and had been receiving shock treatment. This particular day I went with my mother to see him. The hospital was painted white, but a long time ago. It was more cream now with the years of living imprinted on the walls. We came to a wall which had bars on it and a nurse came along. She had a set of keys and she unlocked the door. We began walking down the corridor. There were a number of people in this hospital. I was quite young, about eight. We passed cells of people. You could see them in the rooms in white strait-jackets. My father was in a ward at the end of the corridor. I could not understand the feelings I had here. I focussed on waiting to see my father. Immediately I saw him I ran to him. It was his birthday. I had brought him some liquorice which was his favourite. He had been in hospital for some time. I hadn't yet understood that it would be some time longer before he would be home. We visited as usual for an hour and a half and my mother told me it was time to leave. From within I could feel an enormous burst of need and I ran to him and threw my arms around him and said,

"Daddy, why can't you come home. Why are they keeping you here?"

As I saw this vision within my mind I felt enormous pain within my heart. I couldn't understand why my father, who had always been there for me, who had always put me to bed at night, whose love I'd always felt like a warm sunbeam, all of a sudden was not in my life. As I connected with him in this hug, I re-connected to the warmth of the bodily touch I needed. I could feel the fire in his blood, that feeling that I loved so much. He said, " It's okay love, it's the best thing."

Somewhere deep within me though, I didn't understand, I was too young. I could sense that it must be right because he said so and I trusted him. I left with my mother.

The pain I felt was very deep and as I sat feeling this toothache I cried and cried. I was beginning to face the deep pain I needed to see within me and the more pain I felt the more I cried and the tooth pain began to ease.

"Isn't there some other way I can learn?" I said to the tooth. "Sometimes," it said, "you won't listen and we have to revert to such means to get your attention. Begin to listen, be aware and the way will become easier."

I knew within me that another healing process was beginning. These were some of the leaves that were growing on the plant that

I was watering. They had come from the seeds of healing. I was giving it space and time and I had to give it more space and time. I could feel the process was well underway. I'd been fortunate my father was still alive and well. I am able to love him now and feel love from him. Still, there are pains from my childhood that need love and light in order to heal. I am aware that as the leaves unfold in this healing plant that grows within me, so too do the flowers and fruits of that tree. Everytime I get understanding from a leaf I know the fruit and the flowers are not far away. That is why the little girl inside thinks she can never get what she wants because she wanted her father so much and wasn't allowed to have him. But she does have him now. He is within her and comes as an aspect of herself that she can develop. It is for me to teach her that and to show her that by bringing in those qualities of protection and caring. Although my father is still alive and well and loving I cannot expect him to heal the child within me now. I began to realise I have to be now as a grown up, both my mother and father. I have to love myself, protect and care for myself and provide a space for myself in the world. I am no longer a child, my father is no longer ill and I must come forward into the now for that is all there is. Let go of my past in order that it may heal and so allow myself to move into the present and future, in a full positive loving way. Being parent to my own child, I walk hand in hand with my Mother, Father God Self.

*　　　*　　　*

He sat there for hours in his pyjamas and dressing gown, sometimes sitting in the sun, sometimes in the rain and wind. Nothing about him seemed to change. I wondered what went on in his head, what thoughts he had in all those hours spent in silence. I sat with him. The pigeons were flying all around. It was a sunny day. There were pigeons of many colours; black, white, blue cross, red check,

95

madenas and fantails. They were quite a pleasure to watch. The sun shone brightly this day. The sky was a rich, clear blue. There were other bird sounds coming from the bush behind the house. The stillness of the bush pervaded the back yard. It was indeed quite pleasant, just sitting, being. I was ten now and curious. I wanted to know more.

"Are you alright, Dad?" I asked. It was a way of trying to find out what was happening. He sat still for a long time. No answer came. An hour passed. I sat with him going through my own feelings of not having my question answered and coming to the point where I felt at peace with that. He replied. "Yes."

The reply came almost as a shock, but it came with great assurance even though that was not given in the tone of the word itself. I felt enormous gratitude that I had been answered and that, indeed, he was alright. It didn't matter what were his thoughts. It mattered only that he was content with them. I felt happy at that.

It seemed that reply was the answer that I remembered in the years that followed, no matter what was happening in our family life. I knew somewhere within that all was alright. One answer, one word, spoke a thousand.

Chapter 16

SILVER SPOONS

I had wanted to try one of these sessions for a long time. I had heard that people got insights about who they might have been in the past. The whole idea about Reincarnation excited me and I knew that even if I found not a past life that I would find something perhaps of this lifetime that I needed to understand about. I went to the room in the house where this was to take place. It had a different feel from the other rooms and was filled with mandalas and shamanic type trinkets, pictures of birds flying, feathers and stones of many colours. The people seemed nice. They worked together, man and woman. I noticed that the woman, whom I later came to know well, was adorned with much New Age jewellery; much of it silver with stones of various kinds embedded in it. She seemed to glow. As she was talking with me I felt her warmth. I felt at ease with the man also. They seemed quite connected and quite different; one giving a nurturing energy, the other a protective one. I was glad they were both there. I settled down after talking for some time with them, and lay on the bed. Crystals were placed upon my chakras.

I felt sensations of pulling energy, like force-fields and I felt myself entering other worlds. I could see myself but I was not human. I had thick red skin and I was part mammal, part amphibian, it seemed. I sat on rocks and was equally able to swim underwater without requiring air for long periods of time. The most noticeable thing was the incredible sense of telepathy I had with others like me. There was no need for speech for all understood everything, everyone understood everyone else's thoughts almost to the point where there were none. There was the sense of complete Oneness with everyone. The skin was thick and hard, primitive, like in nature and the physical life seemed that primitive. No houses nor creature comforts of any kind, the basic planet made of rock with some water. The people on this planet seemed to have no needs, when food was required, it was there. Far from primitive, it was more advanced than anything I could remember or anything I felt that I'd ever known.

I came back to daily consciousness aware of a part of me that knew everything and that has wisdom beyond anything of which I could conceive. I could see an expansive consciousness beyond time and space as I know it now. I felt as though I had no needs. I felt every cell in my body vibrate.

No sooner was I back than I went again to another place, another time, which cannot be described as place and time but to a place within where I asked for help from my inner, to understand what I needed to know.

I was presented with an image of a can of paint, it seemed to come thrusting forward and I asked my Higher Self,

"What am I supposed to do with this?"
"Open it!"
"How, with what?" and a crowbar came towards me with as much speed and thrust as the paint.

"Open it!" it said again. It seemed strange in a way, that the force of the voice and the power of the voice was one that I instinctively trusted. I saw myself opening the tin. I found inside a mostly blue paint. In the top corner of the tin there seemed to be a fungus, full of maggots. I felt somewhat repulsed by what I saw. "What are you showing me this for?" hoping to make sense of all this ludicrousness.

98

"Well this is what you are doing to yourself," it said, "Can't you see?" "In what way, how?" I began to feel as if I was falling into another time, another dimension and saw myself as a child in this lifetime. I was eight years old and I saw the bedroom that I lived in at that time. A very clear vision of the dressing table, the drawers and the handles. It was an old dressing table that had been my Aunty's. It had two very long drawers. I saw myself putting jam sandwiches in the drawers. They had been made by my mother for my lunches.

"I don't understand" I said.

"Keep looking." The voice said. The instinct that I felt within made me follow the process. I then saw my mother's hands opening the drawer. The drawer by this time was completely full of jam sandwiches and then the memory had returned. I had hated jam sandwiches. I saw myself at school at lunch time after I had drunk the milk provided by the government in those wax paper cartons. I'd go to open my lunch and I'd be embarrassed. It seemed others would have things I would rather have and so I would spend my bus money on some food in the canteen or go without if I was to be driven that day, rather than to be seen with jam sandwiches. I took to leaving them behind before I came to school. Again the vision came, my mother's hands ready to open the drawer. She opened the drawer and the maggots and flies flew out. She screamed,

"What have you done?"

"It's the jam sandwiches," I said, "I didn't want them." I felt very afraid, very guilty, as if I had done the wrong thing. My mother responded and I was shocked at her response.
"Why didn't you tell me? I would have made you something different."

I began to feel that travelling fast feeling again and the Higher Self voice higher in my consciousness and recognition was coming of something I hadn't conceived, that I actually had choice, I could say what I wanted and perhaps receive it.

I didn't have to accept anything. I could make the statements about what I wanted. The memory came back after that time. My mother did start making me different things for lunch each day and sometimes giving me money for lunch so that I could buy from the canteen without having to walk home. I remember it seemed a totally new consciousness to me, even then, that I didn't have to be dictated to by the world. I began to see that I needed to take power again, in my life and make decisions to say what I wanted. To be aware that to some degree at least, I was master of my own destiny and there were certain choices which I could make that could make changes in my life for which I was looking. I began to feel a sense of responsibility for my own life.

The voice continued, "Well, that's right. It's time you started to ask for what you want."

Still, in my consciousness I could feel some resistance. "If you really wish to be with another man, then let yourself be. You don't have to be with a man just because he's there." I felt shocked and this felt like waves of shell cracking around me. What I was being told was almost inconceivable to me. I had felt that I had to settle for what I had, to be grateful and I had spent some time learning that. It was also a necessary part of my development but the time had come where I had tried hard enough to no avail. I had been in a relationship for some time which had begun to cause me a great deal of inner unhappiness. It just didn't seem to move or get anywhere. I felt thwarted at every turn but because of this sense that I should accept and be grateful for what I was given I remained stagnant, making no move to change the relationship or the life that I was in. To become aware that I could take the reins of my own chariot and steer it on a course better suited to my needs was a huge realisation for me and it seemed to be coming into me on a cellular level. I could feel every cell within me changing structure, changing thought, changing form. It seemed that I was being shown surprise after surprise.

"If I am supposed to make this change," I said, "How do I do it?" In the same way as the paint tin and the crowbar had been presented two silver spoons came forth.

"Here." It said. "Put one in each hand." I could feel a deep laugh within me and yet another realisation within me about people getting life presented to them on a silver spoon. They could have everything they wanted and here was I. I had not one but two silver spoons. I knew that my consciousness was changing to embrace this reality.

At this level and vibration I could not only feel it but I knew it. This is how they worked, the Light Beings, they would raise you in consciousness to such a fast vibration and drop in a new thought form, a seed, that could become a way of perceiving the world. When the healing is over and the human being returns to daily consciousness, daily awareness, that seed still sits within the aura and begins to grow. Changes take place within the person's life as the seed grows and develops at the pace with which the person can cope, a pace with which the person can grow and understand. The seed had been planted within me and life began to change.

Before the session ended I asked why was the paint blue. This was to be the clue for my next step.

"It is the colour of Mother Mary. The Mother energy. Paint yourself with it. Nurture yourself, for that is what you need. When you refuse to take in the Mother energy, it is then you start to rot within, for you become out of alignment and undernourished. Immerse yourself in this blue paint, this blue light. Let it replenish and heal you."

I knew that I had to begin to give to myself. I had spent much of my life giving to others and I could see that the giving had come from a place of martyrdom. It was time for me to change that. I had to stop trying to please others, to seek their approval, because of my own insecurities. I had begun to change this by seeing that I was important and I had needs too. It was not for me to expect others to give to me, which is what I had done in my martyrdom. It was for me now to begin to give to myself. No one else could do this, only I and Mother Mary, I had to find the Mother within.

The Pilgrimage

Chapter 17

WHERE EAGLES FLY

Jan. 1989 Putapatti, India

There is peace within and it can be found. One must simply know the right place to look. There are, on this Earth, many teachers who can help us find it. They can only point the way, we must walk there ourselves. Sometimes we don't see the clues even when there are signs everywhere. At other times the sharp reality of truth shines upon us like a flashlight in the dark.

I had been at Sai Baba's Ashram for two weeks. I had watched him day after day when he appeared to the masses, raising his hands in a circling motion. He would pass by. People would scramble towards him to give him letters and stare intensely in the hope that he would give them a glance. I found it hard to understand how this could be spiritual teaching, for I had seen within the ashram so much greed and competition amongst the people there from countries all over the world, sometimes almost inhumane behaviour in the lines to see which line went in first to be seated in front of Baba. On one day there had been a fight between two women arguing about who should sit in the line first. People would push in order to beat the other to the spot, concerned with self and not others. Others would play the martyr and let others before them, neither seemed better than the other. One day in the queue, I was at the head of the line. There was a system whereby the people at the front of the line put their hand in to get a coupon with a number on. This determined the order in which the lines entered Baba's domain and much importance was placed upon this procedure every day. That particular day I was feeling very beautiful inside. I had felt much connection with Sai Baba on the inner planes. When I had arrived at the Ashram he had greeted me and embraced me. It was a spiritual experience but I felt it physically. His presence touched me and I felt safe and secure. From that moment on I was glad to be there. I had been somewhat like an observer for a short time, until every day a little more peace filled me. Every day a little more love shone. Every day a little more compassion was within me. I reached in to the bag of coupons and pulled out the number thirty. I held it up as people did, to the lines behind me to show the people in my line when we would enter. The compassion, love and peace that I had been feeling increased. After some time I realised that we would be second last, the compassion and the love continued to increase. I realised all through my being that when one has inner happiness, external circumstance does not matter. For inner happiness does not change according to outside circumstance. These words came to me then as clear and as fully as I place them here now. I realised that I felt no guilt nor disappointment, I simply had a sense of knowing that all is perfect. It came time to enter, the twenty ninth line had gone in. I stood up and walked towards the opening of the Temple. It seemed filled, so the ladies in charge directed us towards the front and we made a new line at the front of everyone. Again there was no change in my state, no exhilaration, for I was exhilarated enough in just being and accepting what is.

Sai Baba came by and again he made the circular motion with his hands raising them higher and higher. I watched. As I watched I saw two eagles descend around Sai Baba and commence circling him. They were live eagles, real birds, physically flying. As his hands motioned higher, they circled higher and higher. This activity continued for some time. With his hands he motioned, with their wings they flew, until they were two specks high in the sky. I became aware that as I had just witnessed this, my consciousness, too, had risen with every circling motion. I had lifted with the eagles, higher and higher in consciousness. I could see that Sai Baba was lifting me, as he had been lifting the people for days on end, to higher wisdom, higher understanding. It all made sense, why the lines, why the greed and competition, the self concern and the martyrdom. These were some of humanity's weaker points manifesting within the ashram and there was a way-shower for all to see every day. People could listen, people could learn but they had to choose that themselves.

It seems we have choice. the roads are there, the signs clear but we must choose to walk the way. It was becoming clearer to me that my way was the Way of the Heart. I began to understand that what I had seen as observer in the Ashram in the earlier days was a reflection of aspects of my own being. My own greed, my own self concern and martyrdom. I became aware that self concern and martyrdom go hand in hand, that they are actually polar opposites of each other. When the scales would swing too far in one direction and one's own behaviour begins obviously staring one in the face, the tendency is to jump to the other end quickly to balance it out. I had done this for years, in relationships especially, and could change in an instant from one interaction to another. On no occasion, in these instances, coming from a full and loving heart. That was clear, if hard to see in myself. But it was the truth and a part of myself with which I had to come to terms. I began to understand that motive mattered.

Not far from the Ashram, in the town of Putapatti, there was a beautiful hill. In the hill was a wishing cave, where, everyone said, whatever you wished for came true. I had looked forward to going to this wishing well. I had met a man before I had journeyed to the Ashram for whom I felt a strong passion, and he lived at the opposite end of the world. I thought, as I had thought about what

I could wish for, that I would ask that we could be together. I walked to the hill with this in my mind. I was yearning inside for his touch. The journey took some time and I enjoyed watching the villagers and the Indian children along the path. There were bison. There was a watering hole. The valley of a river was only sand and patches of water where the villagers bathed. It was a hot day and the sun beat down strongly. I was with a group of friends, all a part of the group from Australia and Denmark to which I belonged. Together with this small group I meandered up the hill, feeling like a goat. The way was steep and large steps were required to climb the rocks. I enjoyed this activity and I could feel the adventurer within me. When we arrived at the mouth of the wishing cave I sat for a moment in quiet contemplation and thought again that I would ask to be connected with this man. As I walked towards the cave and placed my head within it, I could feel myself lifting in vibration and I could no longer ask for what I thought I would wish for. For the rise in vibration took me to another plane so high, that words came as my wish that were greater than anything I'd ever conceived of before. It had to do with peace. It had to do with the Hierarchy descending, bringing light to the earth. It went greater than that. I caught a glimpse for a millisecond of the expansiveness that goes beyond the universe itself. I came away from that cave feeling at One. As I descended the hill I wondered why I hadn't been able to ask for my wish. I tried again on several occasions when I came to the wishing cave and every time the same result. I began to see that my motive was not right, that my concern was with myself, my needs and desires and that I could not ask this of God. For to ask this was to ignore the Divine Plan. I realised the necessity for the words " according to the Will of God." I felt that, whilst I recognised this, God's Will, I would want for nothing. The yearning, the desire for touch and the need within me diminished. I could feel the embrace of spirit within, nurturing every cell, every organ, every limb and I could feel the expansiveness of my heart, as I opened, to not just this one man in my consciousness, but to all people at every moment, trusting that every need would be met, whether I understood it or not. I felt I could fly as high as eagles and beyond.

I had journeyed to this Ashram as part of my own pilgrimage. Some years earlier, when guided into meditation by the Lady Shan Tara, I saw the inner Ashram from which I came. To my amazement, in my inner, I saw the Lady Shan Tara and three men. One was Sai Baba, although I had never seen his picture in this lifetime, another Shirdi Sai and the third is still not recognised. I was excited by this vision within and soon after went to live in a new household with new people. One of the people in the house had a picture in their bedroom of Sai Baba and I recognised him from my inner vision. I was not used to such experiences at this time and found myself quite amazed at all this psychic phenomenon. In my vision he was dressed in orange and he was channelling energy in my direction. Standing behind him was Shirdi Sai, his predecessor, of whom I knew nothing at that time. It took some years after discovering who Sai Baba was before I journeyed to his Ashram for there were many other things for me to learn where I was. I had learned much from the journey, it was indeed timely, and I also found a much deeper connection to Shirdi Sai and the line of Siddhas from which he comes. When I entered the Temple, the second day at Sai Baba's ashram, I saw the photograph of Shirdi Sai and the memory of the meditation with Lady Shan Tara returned. There was a connection with all of them and I was just beginning to see it.

I went to the Temple every morning at four, walked around the Temple three times and entered. For some days my meditations had been quite strong and I was told little things to do for the day. I was beginning to enjoy the routine and felt I had grown quite a lot in the short time that I had been there. I wondered what more there was to learn. I had many memorable experiences in the ashram. They served to awaken my heart; I shared a beautiful connection with a close friend, our love for each other seemed to blossom in this atmosphere. She, a woman of sixty eight years and me a woman of thirty. We had moments of laughing together as if we were children, beautiful belly laughs that brought tears to the eyes, rolling incessantly down the cheeks. I had slept in the sheds under the mosquito nets which reminded me of my childhood in Queensland in the heat and brought great delight to me. Many beautiful things I had experienced. My heart was preparing to open more.

Chapter 18

THE TOUCH OF A GURU

Feb. 1989 Ganeshpuri, India

Her face had drawn me for some time. It was the last thing I expected right now, but there it was, large as life, telling me it was time to come. The first time I met her she danced in my heart, enthusiastically, gracefully and I could feel her touch like feathers come in a breath of wind. It was not a physical but a spiritual reality manifesting in Presence. It had been an intensive weekend and though short she had made her mark upon my heart. She had now space within it that would remain forever. The marble floor felt hard beneath me. I was tired and at four thirty in the morning my body only just awake I could feel the weight of my bones and hips pressing hard against the marble floor, my spine uncomfortable, my inner fidgety. Her presence brought calm and behind her face was Sai Baba telling me.

"Yes you must go to her. It is time."

My rational brain started counting the days left in India, the finances, the distance to travel. I knew that even though the days left and the finances were short and the miles long, it made no difference, for the call had come and I responded. It was the Mother energies calling, coming to balance the masculine within me. I journeyed.

I felt a yearning to satisfy a part of me that had been crying out for some time; to walk on the beach, to swim with the fish, to play in the sun. Goa called that part of me, a small seaside town on the west coast of India. I thought that I would head there on the way and did so. The time there was short but necessary to calm aspects of my being which had felt unheard. I swam, I sunbaked, played volleyball. I met many people from many countries and shared evenings in the moonlight, dining and sharing. The call came again, impatient now that I had sunken into solitude and would not listen. I asked many people if they knew the way to Gurumayi's Ashram. I could not find the way. Finally something registered and I made the decision within that I was to go regardless. I prayed for help.

The help came the following day. I began heading for the bus to go North to Bombay. As I was going, bags packed and hopping into the taxi, a woman whom I had seen some days earlier, felt an urge to connect with but disregarded it, came towards me. She asked if she could share the ride. I was glad of her company. Once arranged and moving towards our departure point we began a conversation.

"Where are you going?"
"I'm actually trying to get to an ashram. I know it is near Bombay. It's Gurumayi's ashram. I haven't found anyone who can show me the way, so I'm just going."

She smiled, a look of knowing and opened her bag pulling out a magazine with a picture of Gurumayi on the front. She opened the page and the title read. "The Ashram and how to get there." She passed me a pen and paper and said,

" You've got five minutes. Write it down quickly."

I took the instructions. It involved taking a train from Bombay to a small town, then catching a bus. I jotted it down quickly and the woman within seconds of my finishing stopped the cab and jumped out. A feeling of exhilaration filled my being. I was again on track.

I have come to know that when I am most aligned is when I am most tested. The test followed quickly on the heels of this connection. I bought my ticket for the bus to Bombay, a twenty four hour journey and stood amongst many other Indians and some travellers like myself waiting for the bus. I made friends with some girls from Canada. We bought a mango and a drink which we shared in the heat of the sun. There were several buses leaving for Bombay within half an hour of one another. The bus drivers came for the tickets. I was waiting to see which bus was mine. One by one those whom I had spoken to and made friends with hopped onto buses and drove off leaving me with the last bus, which was by all accounts the least attractive. There was no air conditioning, not much padding on the seats and it was aged beyond the years of the others by at least twenty. Holding my breath as I had learned to do in India at times, I passed my bags to the driver. They were thrown underneath with the others and I found my seat on the bus. I was the only white woman, indeed the only woman on the bus. The bus was filled with a group of men who seemed to know one another, who had done a film together, shot on location. They were in high spirits and were quite congenial towards me. I was polite, yet alert underneath, aware that I needed to keep my wits about me for this journey.

We came to a town in one of the Indian districts on the way where the bus pulled over and everyone got out. They went into a liquor store where they bought a licence and liquor. No sooner were we off again when the bottle tops were opened. The smell of alcohol permeated the bus. Very rapidly the energies changed and I felt somewhat irked by their behaviour. Even more aware now to keep my wits. I was clothed in such a way that every part of me was covered, no body line, very much like a sack, only my own showing forth that I was foreign. I attempted to curl up to sleep with little success due to the bumpiness of the roads and the ricketiness of the bus itself. The man beside me kept falling all over me, purposely I felt. I prayed within for strength to get through this journey in one piece. I was tired and knew I could not rest. Within an hour it began to get dark. There were a few hurdles left, I knew, as I was hungry and we had not yet stopped at some of the outpost eating houses along the way. I had to find a toilet and get back on the bus, as well as eat. All of which seemed a huge hassle in such a culture. I did this and feeling a little more confident and relieved tried to settle into sleep. The lights went out and within moments I felt a grabbing, clutching, grovelling hand at my crotch. I reacted more quickly than I would have known possible, managing to grab the arm connected to the hand and stood up. I let go, in full volume, for the man to "lay off!". I took him by the throat and looked into his eyes with such vehemence that he sat down shamefully. Many others apologised for this man's behaviour. I knew now I really could not rest. For the rest of the journey I continued praying, asking for protection, for help until the journey ended many hours later. When I arrived in Bombay I was a mess, overly stressed inside and out. I booked into a hotel that I could afford and had to wait four hours for the room. When I finally got in I threw off my clothes and lay on the bed asking again of God "Why?" and in all earnestness for the first time, I was ready for the answer. It came. I sat up and looked at myself in the mirror. In my eyes I could see more than me. They were cold and hard and calculating and I felt as if there were two of me now, one observing and one being that coldness that I could perceive. It was as if I was possessed, yet it was me or at least it had been invited by me, this entity. It was there as large as life and it yielded a lot of power. I saw my body in the mirror with eyes that I had accused men of having, as if they were looking at a pornographic magazine. I could feel the energy of lust and desire and a quality of voyeurism, all within me. I decided to play with this energy, to let it run, to find its source, to know it and to accept it. I allowed it to take control. The observer was still strong and curious and watched aghast as the energy moved. It seemed it was a being all to itself with its own fulfilment its only aim. It was living off me and I had allowed it. I asked within what I could do to release this being. I was told that I had to let go of my attachment to it. I was aware that it had come to me through men for a long time. Now that I had been without a boyfriend it had come to me directly. I began to wonder if it was this energy that had created the rape in Sri Lanka. We met face to face. I had to face the part of me that had invited it. I prayed for help, for guidance. I even toyed with the idea of staying at the hotel another day to play with this energy until I realised that this was how it had me. I left, having prayed and asked for help knowing that it would come.

I walked into the world. The smells and sound of India began to fill my consciousness and for a time I forgot the exploits of my own inner battle. My task now was to get to the ashram. I found the train station and boarded a train. As the train began its journey I felt a surety, a certainty of purpose. The first stop showed me that the train stations were named in Hindi. The directions I had were in English and I panicked. Whenever anyone entered the train I asked if they understood English. They laughed, offered me fish and shook their heads. I felt a sisterhood and I relaxed in this regardless of my dilemma. I had been on the train for one and a half hours and I knew the stop I needed to be at was soon approaching. A woman entered who not only spoke perfect English but who knew where the Ashram was. She took it upon herself to take me off the train and direct me onto the correct bus, telling the conductor where to let me off. I was safe.

The Ashram itself was a far cry from anything I had experienced before. Its beauty was stupendous, its aura immense. The marble floors, columns and statues were beyond expectation. It was filled with an energy I could sense in every particle of the air. Everything was clean, the gardens full of nourishment and in the heat they were lush and plentiful. Waterfalls flowed making beautiful patterns in the air and coloured lights of natural beauty lined the skies. As I explored the Ashram over the coming days its beauty became more and more imminent, more powerful, there were no disappointments. It just got better. About the fourth day I stumbled across a meditation hill. It was rich with grass and life force that filled the entire body. I went every morning at four and watched every sunrise. I went every evening at five and I watched every sunset. I became one with the life and energy of this Ashram. I could feel the nourishment of the Mother energy intuning every cell of my being. Every interaction, every word spoken with every person, of body language, of movement, every gesture, every vision, every breath of wind, every petal of a bud had meaning.

I met Guru Mayi. She appeared at Darshan. The beauty and femininity that exuded from her being touched my heart again. It was time for me to take Darshan and I did so. Her eyes met mine. I was filled with love so rich and deep and pure that my eyes welled over with tears. I could feel a fullness within me. I was overflowing with the essence of Presence. I felt that I was beginning to understand the word Shaktipat.* She spoke asking me how my back was. I had trouble in the previous days sitting for long hours in meditation and at Sapna, which is the singing of a particular chanting. It was being held in honour of one of her devotees who had died only thirty years old. I loved the singing but battled with my body on the marble floor. I replied to her that my back was fine but I took her meaning. I knew there was something not right about it. She said "It will go soon." Within

116

moments of leaving her presence I felt excruciating pain in my feet and a voice in my head told me, "Your pain is leaving you now."

I went back for Sapna and I sat for hours, no back trouble. When I went to bed that evening, one by one every vertebrae clicked. It woke the whole dormitory. I was embarrassed and very joyful.

The following day I had been meditating some hours and it seemed that the picture of Muktananda spoke to me. It said,

"Go to my shrine for I have a message for you."

I immediately went to the shrine and as soon as I had sat down in meditative position once more the message came.

"Your work is in the West, you must return."

I felt a sadness within but a knowing that it was truth. I had felt that I could be in a place like this for many years and yet would evolve no further. It would be only repeating something I had already done. The voice of Muktananda continued to speak within me.

"You will be cleansed and purified whilst you are here in the next few days. The entity will leave you." I was shocked, for in my holiness I had forgotten the existence of the entity within me that I had discovered in the hotel in Bombay. I couldn't fool my inner and I was glad. I felt relief that my prayers had been answered. The voice outlined the steps I had to take to release it. It told me that the entity could not survive in the light of the Ashram.

"In three days you will leave on the morning bus, your work in the west is waiting."

117

I was shown a picture of Guru Ananda Tara Shan. She had a beautiful smile and welcoming eyes. I knew it was time to return to her and with her that I must work in this lifetime. I was aware that through her I would come to understand something of the Mother energies in their fullness. For now I was to be cleansed and purified of this sexual entity. Muktananda had given me clear instruction.

"You are to go to the Arati prayer in the temple for the next three days. There is a statue of Shirdi Sai in the gardens. Find it. Go to it with the American girl you have met. There is a fire there. Call on the energies of that fire, ask the girl to channel light. Call the entity to you and tell it that it must leave. You must follow all these steps."

Over the following days I followed the steps that had been outlined for me. I discovered the fire and found that it had been burning for one hundred and fifty years in honour of Shirdi Sai. I asked the American girl, Susan, if she would help me. We had spent some time together already, sharing our stories of the path we had journeyed to get to our present level of understanding. I enjoyed her company and would often walk up the hill with her in the early hours of the morning. The day that we were to go to the fire Guru Mayi called everyone to the temple. There was to be a special festival that involved the cleansing of the statue of Muktananda in the temple. The ceremony began. Sanskrit prayers were chanted for three hours. As the prayers were chanted the statue was washed and cleansed and it seemed so was the inner of all present. I could feel the process taking place within me. Time came for Susan and me to go to the fire. As the process of purification took its course, I could feel within me a light so pure, an innocence I had longed for. I called the entity to me and though I could not see it, I knew it was there. I did as Muktananda had told me. The perennial redemptive qualities of that fire began to burn within me. I could again sense the connection of the Siddhas and my time in that in the past. I felt a power of love and connection with spirit that ran deep and in those last days at the Ashram I laughed laughs deep to my core. I really had fun on all levels and could sense the joy of soul. I had been liberated within. When I left on the bus I could sense that I might return one day. It would only be for a spiritual 'refill' if I got too stressed in my work in the West. My life was just beginning. The real work was still to come and I could feel the pull of my homeland and of my Mother Ananda.

Union

Chapter 19

THE HEART KNOWS

I had felt the desire to know my life path. I had, in my earlier years, made many attempts to find that out, through asking others who I believed could see more, or know more than I. This meant that I went to clairvoyants and other such readers of varying kinds in the hope that they would show me my life, that I could somehow escape the pain of letting it unfold. It had seemed painful until now. I gave these people a lot of power in my life, the power to paint whatever picture they fancied of my life. I then proceeded to help the painting manifest by becoming everything they told me that I would become. Enormous power I gave them. It was the power I should be giving to my own spirit, my own knowing within, but I was afraid to face the enormity of that. Instead, I played the victim and I played the part well. It was really rather absurd. One of my deepest desires was to find a mate, a partner for this lifetime. I knew within that there was one waiting, I was waiting and I was tired of waiting. Everytime I visited one of these clairvoyants I would ask, "When is he coming?" The answers would be varied but had a general pattern of one or two years. Over the next ten years or so, I went for such readings and the answer remained the same.

"One or two years." It was just a safe enough time to not matter. This meant that no one I was with in a relationship was ever the right one and I was always waiting for my partner to come. Therefore sometimes I couldn't stay with the man I was with, in case the man I was waiting for came along. It affected my relationships severely. It finally came to me that I had to stop looking for Divination from outside of myself, I had to find the knowing within. I had to stop giving power to other people around me whom I saw as more together or more spiritual. I had to take power over what I wanted from life and be responsible for the choices and decisions that I was making. So I did. I decided within me that I only wanted one partner now and I wanted a partner that only wanted one partner too, that was me. This was the turning point, the decision.

I entered a period of time where all my resistances to that decision were threatened. It seemed, all of a sudden, that there were men everywhere wanting to be with me. They all seemed to be working at breaking down my resistance to relationships. I was not prepared to be with anyone for I knew my heart had to be fully involved with the choices that, I became aware, I had to make. I asked my heart what I should do. I wanted God to descend with a neon sign saying " Marry this one!" But God didn't. There had been two that had touched my heart and I was not sure of what I should do. I felt desperate. For months I laboured over the decision. My reasoning mind weighed up the advantages and the disadvantages of each and I could see complete scenarios of life before me for each alternative choice. I put it to my Higher Self.

"Okay, should I marry this one?"
"Well, you can if you want to."
"Well, should I marry the other one?"
"Well, you can if you want to."
"Should I marry someone else altogether?"
"Well you can if you want to." These were not the answers I had hoped for. I was looking within me for the same blanketed divination of the clairvoyants. This was not aligned with the truth so I could not find it. "I don't understand why you won't tell me what I should do, please tell me." The frustration I felt within was becoming enormous. The answer came.

"You see Cheryl, it's like this, you have been given free will in this life and there are certain choices which only you can make. They are your karmic choices and they determine your spiritual destiny, your spiritual evolution, which you are responsible for and which you have to start taking responsibility for. The different alternatives you present lead you along different paths, to a degree, and this is your choice. You must decide that which is the best for all concerned and have that in your heart. You must follow your heart for you walk the Way of the Heart."

The frustration I was feeling began to diminish and I could feel within me a degree of relief for I knew I was being presented, for the first time, with truth in this area. I had allowed the media and society's expectations, that seemed strong within the current of the New Age approach to soul mates, to present me with a picture that was not in alignment with the truth. They overlooked the principles of karmic choice and spiritual responsibility. I had always thought of the betrothals in the East as a strange concept, but I was beginning to see that there was a need for balance in the energy of the choosing of a mate that took these things into consideration. That to make a true decision from the heart, one had to go beyond the want of personality and the thought of satisfaction of desire, to a place where one could choose according to what was the best for the spiritual growth of all concerned. This was where the love came in. This was the role the heart played in sending pure love, unconditional love, to allow union to either take place or not take place according to the Will of God. I could see that I had not to be even attached to the thought that I could marry. I had to let it go and I had to just allow my heart to take the decision at its own pace, without interfering with the mind and without lowering the vibration of love with my unquenched needs and desires. I could feel a lot of shift taking place in all my bodies as this realisation was coming forth. I had been searching for this truth my entire lifetime and here it was plainly evident before me. It was my opportunity now to embrace it and become it.

The higher voice continued,

"All that is asked for is that you follow your heart and the universe will support you in that decision. It will bring energy to the union that you choose because you are important. Your task is important and anyone you choose is important also. You must trust that help will come to form a beautiful union if that is what you truly aspire to from your heart."

"How will I know what my heart wants?" I asked.
"Your heart knows and expresses an inner joy, unrelated to time, space or thought. Allow yourself to go the Way of the Heart."

I could sense that more understanding would come.

Chapter 20

"IN-CARNATION"

I had never seen a landscape like it before. It was how I imagined Ladhark would be in Tibet. There was no sign of plant life and the ground seemed to be made of dust. The colours of the land were dull and grey brown. The colours of the sky were red and rich. I felt uncertain as I stood upon this land. It was not earth as I knew it. It was not earth. I stood for some time, still taking in the landscape. I had read and thought about other planets but never fully considered the reality of their existence. I tried to find something I could cling to, or at least associate with, but there was nothing except sky, an atmosphere which surrounded the planet I was on. I became aware of a pit. I could see beings in that pit, many of them, tall and thinner than humanity. Their skin seemed black and red and their hair was blonde and tufted. The feet were big, the hands webbed. I could see and sense a feeling of inferiority within my being as the thought of approaching these beings was imminent. It was a step I had to take. As I dived into the pit I found myself in water and I knew though it made no logical sense that I also had to enter the fire in that water. I felt it burn me and cleanse me. The beings were helping me and as I emerged from the fire they supported me and helped me to sit down gently beside them. I did not feel inferior any more. I had taken initiation. I began to climb out of the pit feeling at one with this new land, those beings, and I breathed in the Light and felt the fullness of air within me. My face had been painted. I could feel the wind blowing hard upon my face and I felt incredibly strong. I had mastered all things, Fire, Water, Air ...

I landed on Earth with a thud. It was a shock. I saw myself heading towards it. It was blue and green, it seemed cold and I felt as if I was being punished. All of a sudden from the feeling of fullness I had felt on what had become my home, I felt empty. I was in Alaska, an Eskimo, I did not understand, food was scarce, survival difficult. Harsh physical conditions, rugged in bear skin, chewing whale blubber, eating seal. I lived a life with one friend and did not know what I had done wrong. I ended the life by diving down a seal hole. The crystalline colour of the ice, white flashed before me as I met death.

I travelled a life further south in America. I could see tall pine trees, and through them, the corn fields, rich lush earth, juicy, yellow corn, with green land all around. Harvest time. A log cabin, a husband, children, a fulfilling life, closeness to the family, to souls I knew well and loved.

Further south still in America, the land red, the earth red, the temperature warm, my skin red. I could feel the spirit around me. I stood firmly, strong within, eagles flying all around, I could tell them what to do, connected with them in spirit. They sat on my shoulder and walked my walk with me on earth, I found connection with spirit once more.

The thud with which I came back to earth was evident in my consciousness. I may even have chosen to come but in taking the step had lost memory of that choosing. In taking form I had lost the consciousness of the choice itself. In ignorance, I thought God had rejected me and for some time I lived in that ignorance. As the circumstances changed I began to think it was not all punishment. In actual reality, whether one finds reward in incarnation or feels it as punishment it is of little consequence to life itself. The purpose of that life can be met regardless. It is how one perceives one's life and one's response to that perception which determines its quality. Nothing else. I began to see that if I could recognise the perfection of all things in the Plan of my life then the quality of life would have its right respect. Seen this way it is much easier to live a full and loving life. One is not weighed down by the burdens and pain that accompanies anger and bitterness and resentment to the Divine for the fact that the incarnation has taken place. Responsibility can be taken for the choice to live and a life can take its right form. A joyous existence can manifest. It is here that we have choice and that the choice can be taken to create a lighter life. I could see that I could no longer remain in ignorance of the responsibility I have in living, for creating my own path and part in the Plan itself. I could not continue to blame God and feel rejected or guilty for the fact that I was on earth in the first place. I could see clearly the error of my previous thoughts and I could no longer cling to rejection as a means to prevent myself finding the perfected being within me. I had been doing that a long time.

My thoughts went to my birth. I remembered again the process of rebirthing. It had helped me gain a lot of understanding about this very pattern of rejection within me. I was attending a rebirthing seminar because I had wanted to know more about myself and why I was like I was. I had felt something was holding me back in life, there was something that I was uncomfortable with about life itself, and I thought this might be the answer. To some degree, it was.

Time came for me to re-experience my birth. The hot tub was heated to the temperature of the womb. With snorkel and mask and a woman to help me, I entered. As I went under the memory returned.

It was a clear Saturday in September. At that time in the city where I was born many people's interest was centred on the football. It was time for the finals. Tickets were hard to come by and that year, my father's favourite team was in the lead. The day I was about to come, they were playing. I could sense the excitement in the air, even though I was in the womb and felt it would be a good time to come into the world. I was not really sure what was going on but felt a beautiful surge of energy rush through me. I felt myself begin to move down the birth canal.

"It's time." My mother let my father know the process of labour was beginning.

"It can't come now. I've got tickets to the grand final, Collingwood is playing." He took my mother to her girlfriend's place and went on his way to the football. I was trying to come out, my mother holding on. I could sense an anger within her but did not understand why it was there. I internalised it. As I tried to make movement and felt myself blocked I began to feel that there was something wrong. I made a decision within that there must be something wrong with me, that I was unwanted. A large part of my consciousness wanted to go backward. I could feel pain and sense my mother's pain. I felt if I could hold back then I would not hurt her. I felt guilt for her pain. I began breathing more regularly through the snorkel. Although I felt uncomfortable and felt quite a bit of anxiety within me, I felt glad that this process was helping me see so much and understand so much about the decisions I had made during my birth. It made lots of sense to me and seemed to give a deeper understanding of the patterns I had already recognised in my life.

A period of time elapsed where I felt a mixture of emotions; thwarted and frustrated for not being able to get out, content to sit still and trust, petrified of what was out there as it was completely unknowable, anger at being held back, determined that I wouldn't go anyway just to spite them, and sensing within me an urge for death rather than life, for I was not worthy of life after all.

I was realising in this process that I was using all the external events of my own birth process to back up all of the patterns that were already existing in me. It seemed I had chosen my parents, and my circumstances very well. I seemed to know my parents on some level. I felt within me a strong urge to bring Love into their lives.

Next thing I knew I was out. The woman who was rebirthing me held my head above the water. I could feel my mouth start to quiver and feel the sense of want within me. I wanted nourishment, but nothing came. I felt incredibly vulnerable and could feel that my mother was not there. I wanted her. I could feel myself making decisions about the world. It is a cold, sterile place. I can't get what I want. There is no nourishment here for me. All these decisions I made from this event of birth. More time elapsed where I felt varying emotions around these decisions, until finally, I found myself connected and content in the arms of my mother. The Love and bliss I felt were all encompassing. It was so beautiful to be re-connected to this feeling. As I lay in the arms of this woman, I felt the love of my mother, so full, so complete.

My father entered. The energy of love I felt was withdrawn and I could feel instead anger. My mother was angry. I couldn't understand it. I wanted to tell her there was no need for that, couldn't we just all feel the love? But somewhere within me I learned that the presence of men produces anger and the energy of love is withdrawn. I put that deep into my unconscious and allowed it to affect my relationships with men from that day on. There was much I had to learn. If I was to bring Love into the world I had set up some pretty strong barriers to its Presence in my life. And like many of my generation, I also brought with me some very handy circumstances and parents that I could blame.

For some time I used the rebirthing process as a means of expressing much of the pent up energy within me, still blaming my parents and the world for the way in which I had been treated. Gradually, however, I came to realise that it was I who had set the circumstances in the first place and I who could change them now, the minute I decided to change my thoughts around rejection. In doing this I could let go of all the anger and bitterness around my supposed rejection, and once more see the world in a new Light. I could take responsibility for myself and move forward in life, no longer thwarted by my own negative thoughts that I am not worthy of life. The words of the woman who rebirthed me came back strongly to my consciousness,

"Breathe. It is safe to breathe. There is plenty of air for you!" Life can indeed be full. I must simply choose to let it be.

*　　　*　　　*

Sometimes, it felt easier to split off from life rather than face all this processing. It really was easier not to feel the emotions and thoughts about life. After all, to be one with Light was the important thing, wasn't it?

……. I had begun to like meditation so much that I didn't ever want to come back to life on earth. The inner experiences that I had were so rich that daily life seemed mundane in comparison.

I began to be drawn upwards and felt the expansion of the cells within me until I could no longer feel the presence of my physical body. I was one with light, one with spirit. There was another with me in the room. The feeling within was so beautiful. I wanted

so much to share that feeling but I felt that I had no body, no voice with which to communicate with. I tried to speak, the words would not come. I could feel only light. The desire to communicate was strong within me. I felt incredible frustration at being so one with the light I could not make that communication of the feeling I was having. I tried to use my vocal chords and nothing came.

I began to realise that without form, spirit cannot manifest and began to feel gratitude for the voice and body I have. I could see that spirit was showing me the necessity of the physical body and I felt incredible gratitude that I had one. A vehicle through which light and love could be expressed. What good is spirit if it cannot manifest on earth. Life is eternal. Love is eternal. Life is immortal. It comes in various forms and manifestations which need to be respected on all levels. Sometimes when one has to learn the value of a thing, the thing is taken, so that the lesson can be learned. Life and love are sometimes taken so that we can learn their value. When we recognise their value and the eternal qualities they display, we do not see them as being taken away any more. Instead we live in gratitude that they are given and we respect them for the time we have them. I began to feel again the physical body, the sensation of light within gradually decreased and I found myself to be grateful to be on earth.

*   *   *

Anne had come for her appointment. I did not know exactly what she wanted but had hoped I could help her. I had not met her but had felt warm towards her when she rang. She sounded as if she needed help. "I felt you could help me. There's a man who I feel wants to speak with me and I feel he can come through you." She said, convinced that this was so. I felt a little uneasy for this was not the sort of work I did, nor did I want to begin it now.

133

Something made me stay with it. "Alright, if it is so we will see. Otherwise you will have to go elsewhere." Within a few moments, I became speechless. A feeling of heaviness overcame me and I felt extreme grief within. I began to feel male. At the same time I was watching the process and it seemed quite odd. For over half an hour I sat there unable to speak to her but was aware I wanted to communicate. I felt I should stop but the feeling of heaviness continued. I found myself beginning to speak.

"I didn't want to leave you. I intended to come back. When I was in Thailand I took a boat trip on a small yacht. I didn't take my passport or anything as I thought it'd be a quick trip. The boat overturned. I drowned. I held on to a piece of wood for a very long time, but eventually lost my strength. I really was intending to come back. I love you."

I could feel enormous grief within me. Anne burst into tears. "I knew it! I knew you wouldn't have done it on purpose. Everyone said you were frightened to marry me and took off. They all think you're off in some other country. You're listed as a missing person. I was sure something else had happened."

I could feel her relief and the huge relief of the man within me. This seemed really strange but it was all too real to be worried about that now. I moved towards Anne and we held each other, both of us crying. So much release was taking place.

"I am dead though, Anne. You'll have to let me go now. I've hung on so that you know I love you but I'm being called elsewhere now. I don't like that guy you've been seeing. I don't think he's good for you. But don't worry, there's another one on the way." I couldn't believe these words were coming out of my mouth. I knew nothing about her.

"Promise me you'll let me go now. I don't understand why this has happened any more than you. I only know I'm being called somewhere else and God is sending someone else your way. He's just what you need."

Anne was in deep tears.

"Yes. Yes. I promise! I love you too."

With that, he disappeared and I felt myself in my own body once more.

I didn't know what to say or do. Anne hugged me and thanked me many times. I knew this was not to be my work but I knew for this time it was right. I could sense the release it had brought to these two souls. For my part, I had learned once again that the universe goes far beyond anything I can imagine. I could feel the Joy in my heart as once again I could see that all is perfect in the Plan.

Chapter 21

UNION

There's a saying that if something is yours, you should set if free. If it returns you know it's yours. If not, it was never yours in the first place. This was the approach I had to take in trying to decide as to whether or not I would marry. I had to let go of my attachment to marriage as such and to allow the universe to bring that to me if it was to be so. I had learned from my previous experiences not to ask for a particular man but to ask instead, that what occurs in my life be for the highest good of all concerned. This rapidly became my heart prayer: to aim for nothing but the perfect unfolding of the Plan.

I was finding union with the Divine more and more constant in my daily life and the words "as above, so below" began to echo within me. The union I felt in the light of the Father/Mother God Self was all encompassing, all embracing. From the day that I had awakened within the hospital I knew that, in order to love others, I had to love myself. However, there is always room for improvement in this area as the growth of love is never ending. I realised I had come a fair degree in obtaining this end and was still in process. Also, I now needed to incorporate giving to others as the necessary outflow to balance the inflow I was receiving from the Divine. I could hear the voice of God within me: "You keep up the outflow. Let me take care of the inflow."

Various experiences came my way in general day to day life where I had to trust this. It was mirrored sometimes in the state of my financial affairs and sometimes in terms of positivity I could radiate to others. I became aware of the Law of Karma and Cosmic

Justice, the need to be responsible for what I gave, to give and never count the cost. As I began to live by this Law more and more I could feel the reward of the inflow, sometimes from unexpected sources but always there.

One aspect of this inflow came in the form of a man. When I met him all I could see was a beautiful jewel trapped inside an empty shell. I felt he very much needed love. At that time my concern was to give that love and I was unaware of the gifts the jewel would give me. As I worked at helping him remove the shackles of his past and meeting the need of love within him, I found that the shackles of my own past also fell away and my own needs of love began to be met in a way I did not expect. My motive was not to meet my own needs, and so they were met. At first I found it difficult to comprehend that in giving from a pure heart, one could receive so much and so fully. The longer I knew him the more the jewel within him shone and the light of compassion and love radiated from within me.

When I looked into his eyes, I could feel an energy of protection and dependability, something solid and eternal, as infinite as the universe itself. This look gave birth to an understanding of the perennial fire that burns within the heart and I knew within me what it was to see through the eyes of the heart. Judgement and reason began to take a secondary role and stopped being the controlling influences of my life. They took to them new qualities and found a new context within which they could function. As faculties they were still helpful but they were only faculties. Through this relationship I came to understand much more of goodwill and of harmlessness. Justice, compassion, love and peace, respect and humility all began to take new meaning.

In order to live in harmonious day to day life with Greg, these qualities had to be understood and applied in practice. I was aware that if I was to generate on earth the light I now felt on the inner levels in my meditations and spiritual practices, I had to begin to live the principles and the Divine laws of which I was becoming aware. In meeting Greg I was filled with joy, for here was an opportunity to externalise the inner world and make it tangible. It was a way in which I could be an example for others, as well as to make concrete my inner learnings on a physical level. I found more and more awareness of the need to bring spirit into matter. I had seen when I left the hospital, that heaven is here and I had wanted to bring forth that understanding to humanity. In order to bring it to humanity it had first to become real to me on all levels. I was beginning to see, now, its truth, not only as a spiritual insight but as a physical reality. The need to marry spirit with matter was evident.

I made the decision from the heart, to marry Greg and I knew that That marriage was a reflection of an inner choice to marry with Divinity. On all levels I experienced much joy. No sooner had the decision been made within, than the shadow, the fear, showed itself.

His name was Alexus. He wore a blue coat with white double breasted buttons. I was to marry him. It was during the Revolution. That night there was to be a ball. I was excited and my ladies helped me tie up my corset, pulling it tightly across my waist. I could feel the buxomness of my breasts and I sucked my cheeks to make them go pink. I couldn't decide which dress to wear. I finally opted for the pink and hurried downstairs to meet him. I could see the carriage in the distance, his driver sitting up front and could feel the excitement rise within me as it approached. The servant came to announce his arrival. I nodded that he should be allowed in. The fire was burning and we sat together for a short time on the settle. I felt the fire within my being race whenever we touched and felt nervous and embarrassed. I tried to make conversation and found it easy to speak with him. I so much enjoyed the moments we had alone but I was careful to not allow that eye contact to be too long for fear of where it might lead.

We alighted the carriage and journeyed to the ball. It was held in a huge palatial style ballroom in one of the houses of the aristocracy. Many people were attending, everyone was wearing a mask. We had put ours on some moments before entering. It seemed to create an air of expectancy and curiosity. It was difficult to tell who was whom.

The dancing began. People were paired, the steps were deliberate and precise. It was important to know the steps and to perform them accurately. So much concentration took place as the dance was executed. I could feel an energy rising within me. I was liking this man more and more. He had asked for my hand in marriage and it was three weeks until our wedding. I could hardly wait. I felt as though the reins I had put upon myself, my desires and passions could be released once this marriage took place. My family had not been sure as this man's reputation had been questionable but my father had said yes because he saw the desperation within me. I went to get some punch and found some female friends with whom I chattered. We talked of many things but especially the preparations for the wedding. I could feel their envy. When I finished the conversation I went to look for Alexus and could not find him anywhere. There were people everywhere, on the balcony, on the lawns. I met James and he told me that Alexus had gone to the shed. I headed in that direction full of anticipation wanting to share with him the plans I had made for the wedding. My walk broke into a run. I thought perhaps he was at the stable for he loved horses as did I. I entered the barn and I saw him. It was not as I had expected. I could see his figure nestled amongst the hay, beside him lay a woman. I could not see who, all I could see was the petticoat, the dress lifted around the waist and the naked lower bodies of both. I turned and ran feeling the energies within me imploding upon themselves - the knots I felt within my stomach were all I was conscious of and my mind began to race in hysteria. "The bastard!" I thought "How could he?" - tears streamed down my face. I ran to a carriage that was waiting outside the ballroom. "Take me home!" I yelled, "Take me home!"

Days later he called. I refused to see him. Letters arrived. I threw them in the fire unread. I was angry and I was full of pride. As months passed, I missed him and began to think that maybe I should listen. I asked my ladies to help me dress and could feel the energy of excitement once again. I journeyed to the town where I knew that he would be. I was nearly ready to alight from the carriage when I looked out and saw him. He was walking along in a sprightly manner, head held high, laughing jovially. Beside him was a woman, his arm was placed around her waist and he was talking with her as he had done with me months earlier. I felt sick and I asked the driver to continue. Years passed. I heard reports that he was drinking. He had written letters which I had read, begging me to return. He said he loved me. He said the other women didn't mean anything. I was full of pride. I married a steady man, much older than I, one on whom I thought I could rely. I felt no love, no passion, just security.

When I was old I sat on the rocking chair on the balcony. A letter arrived. Alexus had died from sclerosis of the liver. He had taken to drink. Tears welled. I had not let myself love again. I had loved only him. The pain I began to feel within me was enormous. I spent the rest of the lifetime avoiding feeling the state of grief within me. It was as though I had a permanent knot in my stomach. The lifetime had been wasted, all because of my pride, my inability to look within my own heart and find forgiveness. The grief I did feel served as a further barrier to the love from the man I had married. It seemed nothing could penetrate the heart centre, it was totally closed down to love, surrounded with unexpressed grief and pride.

I was frightened of the love I had for Alexus and I had used my pride as an excuse not to enter it. I could not find forgiveness within me. I had made the choice to settle instead for something predictable and secure, but it had no heart and I knew when I read the letter that I would never do that again, for the lifetime had been one without the love of life itself. The passion and fullness I had felt from being together with Alexus had died and I couldn't help wondering how much fuller life would have been had I gone to him and forgiven him. I knew that he had never loved another and I knew that it was his fear of love, our love, that had instigated the actions that he took that had lead to his alcoholism and his eventual death. I vowed within myself that if ever I got the chance again to open my heart in love I would do so. I had to do this now. I had to overcome the fears of opening to love in marriage and I was being given that opportunity now, in my life.

We were in Ireland. The hills extended a long way. They were bald and green and the cobblestone paths seemed to go forever. You could see the sea on the horizon and the lighthouse not far in the distance, flashing regularly. The house was made of cobblestone also, joined together by lime. We had built it ourselves. It had taken some years to make it complete and still it was small. I lived together with him in marriage. I felt completely indifferent to him. Over the years we had grown apart. It had come to the point where I wished he would leave, for to be in close proximity to him was unbearable. My heart was closed, my body language was closed, our communication minimal. It felt as though we were in the middle

of a cold war. He would disappear for days on end. He would go
to the whore house in the next county. I knew because of the way
those neighbouring us would snigger when I went to market, but I
did not care. I preferred that, at least he was gone and I was free
to be. He died of syphilis and I of cancer through lack of touch. A
wasteful existence it seemed, for both, but the choice was ours and
we had chosen to live life with closed hearts.

As I saw this memory within me, I knew that it was time to redeem
these aspects of our past. To let go of pride and bring in humility
and forgiveness. To open our hearts in love and I had to start with
me. To open mine and to see the difference that it made to life
itself, to circumstance and to life-flow. As the fears rose up within
me and I was shown these lifetimes, all became clear. The fear was
of the past. I was hesitant to embrace love because of that fear, but
I could recognise that the fear was born of the past and I could
take courage to change that. The only way out was to open the
heart, to walk the Way of the Heart. There was no other choice.
To remain closed was no longer a choice that I could make. I had
been shown too much to do this now.

It was the days of Avalon once again that had returned to my
consciousness.

I watched him play, his hair brushed forward upon his brow, his
eyes in deep reverence to the notes he played. The sounds that came
from the harp were like the music of the angels. All who listened
felt it. Merlin and Morgaine sat with him listening with joy in
their hearts. I sat in the audience mesmerised by his beauty and
dedication to his art. He was my sweetheart, and I felt we would
marry. That was not to be. Morgaine could see the beauty of his
music and he was taken for training to be a Druid. His heart was
full of Reverence to God. I understood this, as mine was also. But

I still felt the pain that this meant, for when we went for training, our relationship had to end. There was no question that it could be otherwise, and I, too, took the opportunity to be taken for training as a Druidic Priestess. The men and women were kept apart on the isle. There was little more contact in that lifetime, if any. It did not matter, for the Love of God was felt within us both. What more could one ask for? With training, concern with the physical nature became insignificant. Instead one looked towards God and rose above desire.

I could see the lighthouse on the isle. The buildings were plain and even the grass hills were naturally well kept. I could feel myself reverent and pious, aware of the beauty and nature in the life of the isle. I lived for Archangel Michael and kept my focus on that light.

I asked within me, why is this memory here now?

"It will not be as in Avalon, there is no need for you to remain separate. A new sharing begins. In that lifetime you met and wanted to marry, but you both chose to marry God instead, in spite of the personal pain that was caused. You can marry now, as you chose correctly then. In this New Age a good karma returns to you. Your relationship will go to a new level and will please you both. Your fear is that you will be separated again as you were then. Recognise, it is only fear. Your karma is not that. In this Age your training is still taking place, this time it can be done while you are in union. You are embarking upon a journey from which there is no return. You have shown that you have Right Dedication and Perseverance. Take courage and align your heart to the task of spreading the feminine principle. It is a continuation of a task you have already begun. Avalon lives on for all who have eyes to see and hearts to feel.

October, 1989. Melbourne

Together with Greg, hand in hand we took the step to marry, the aisle representing the beginning of the walk we would make together on the Way of the Heart.

The day arrived and as I prepared to meet him I felt again the energy of passion for life, of excitement and joy at union and of purity and innocence within the heart. Hand in hand with faith, trust and courage we arrived at the church. He opened the door and I alighted from the car. We entered the path together that day and have never looked back.

Chapter 22

BEGIN IT NOW

I had had quite an introduction to this world of light, but never had I heard it so clearly as this day. It was an absent healing evening and I had found it quite a beautiful thing to do, to send thoughts to other people to help them. This particular night I sat in the chair and began to tune in. The meditation began and the voice within me also began. It felt so clear and began to affect every part of me.

Begin it now. Everything that you have ever wished to do or be, be it now. Judge not yourself on past merits or faults for you are not what you once were. Go beyond the limited perspective of self. Go beyond the limited perspective of God. Come to know that all things are possible in God's Light. All things.

Give yourself time to contemplate the existence of mankind and your existence as part of mankind. It may seem futile but contemplation brings perspective otherwise forgotten and lifts you out of the little self into a world where there is more perspective. It is important to allow yourself the space to rise in vibration and not to fear that rise in vibration, for when you rise in vibration you take up more space in the world. Many are frightened of that, feeling not good enough, not worthy of space and time as considerations to the self. The more space taken up by beings of Light, the more hope there is for Earth and humanity. Healing can and will occur if people open their hearts to new understandings and philosophies presently descending into the consciousness of Earth.

Let yourself feel the pains you need to feel whatever form that may take. Find insight and clarity and be able to crack that which inhibits the self. Be able to pull away the trappings that encase the self and stop it from experiencing freedom of flight as spirit.

When one refuses to experience pain and suffering, when it is part of one's Dharma, one cuts oneself off from opportunity disguised as loss.

There are many guises, many forms which spiritual teachings appear within and take on, in order to help us grow and evolve more fully. The lengths to which spirit will go are quite phenomenal and it makes evident the littleness of our own minds and wills when compared with the Mind and Will of the Great Spirit.

Present in the Essence of The Great Spirit are humour and intelligence beyond our normal state of knowing. We are sometimes given access to this humour and intelligence, to the higher mind or what some call the Higher Self.

One wonders when it is so superior in understanding and knowledge that it bothers and we fumble in our analysis of self. We struggle to find meaning in messages. We attempt to interpret the message that the Great Spirit gives, sometimes accurately and sometimes not so, and Great Spirit never gives up, never leaves us, except to show us a deeper light, a deeper understanding through our darkness.

As time goes on our little self begins to develop the qualities of faith, trust and courage because of the unending support that encompasses us always in the essence of the Great Spirit, and in time we become one with that Spirit. We become the life force, the enthusiasm and inspiration that is guided and directed by the Angelic Host.

The moments of Oneness we experience fill us with abundance, fill us with hope and the knowing that we never need. Just a spark of this knowing is enough to keep us going in times of doubt, fear, anger and anguish, in the hope that we will not be deserted, that we will not be separated from the Divine.

Yet we are separated and we do grapple with it when we sink to the lassitudes of the lower mind, the lower self. Like children learning to walk we fall time and time again until we learn.

We get perspective of varying kinds by experiencing ourselves in various states of consciousness. Our perspectives change according to where we choose to stand, be it in alignment with the Divinity of ourselves or be it in alignment with the personality self and its many parts. There are many qualities which we can embody and our perspective alters according to the qualities embodied.

Whether we are working with Will, with Love, with Wisdom or with Active Intelligence and how much we are prepared to blend all of these, determines the wholeness of our attitudes and beliefs. Sometimes we hop from one perspective to another, incorporating only a single trait, in order that we may develop and learn about that specific trait and incorporate it on the path to Perfection.

When one decides to join with spirit and cooperate in one's evolutionary process, the world changes and we see it in a new way. A new reality descends and all that we thought we were crumbles before us.

It is a process that is necessary in order that the true reality, that we are One in spirit, may descend and be felt by us. To do this the illusion must be shattered. Humanity lives in illusion and since we define ourselves so much by the world around us, by that illusion, *it is not an easy process for us. In deciding to give credence to the Divine Reality we must throw away all that we have previously seen as reality and start again. Empty the vessel so that it can be refilled again.*

There comes a period of time between when aspirants or disciples take a decision and when they can actually put that decision in motion. It is in that interim period that many doubts and fears come and test and try the decision. It is during this time that many disciples and aspirants give up and desert their posts, for before they can actuate their promise, their pledge, they must be prepared to rid the self of self concern. Will is not always strong enough unless linked to a true desire for selflessness that is in no way linked to the energy of martyrdom.

Gospels are sent forth. People attempt to live by them but while they are theories only, that is, if the person is not at one with the gospel, if it does not come from the person's heart and mind to live and be one with that gospel, then the gospel is of no consequence or value. For people to align with their promise, their pledge, their decision as aspirant, disciple or initiate, they must let themselves become one with that pledge. That means ridding themselves of any aspect of their nature that is not one with that pledge. It is here that the battle between the Light and dark forces begins within the self, that one must meet one's shadow and overcome it.

There is much joy in the soul when the decision is taken and the alignment takes place. The period of time it takes for the alignment to take place once decision has been made varies according to the individual and their karma. One must never compare with others in this, for each has their own time, speed and vibration that determines this.

Be aware that the joy the soul radiates is the only thing with which one needs be concerned. This is not personality joy we speak of, it is an inner sense of accomplishment that comes when a disciple, initiate, or aspirant are in true connection with, and alignment with their Dharma. There can be no comparison to others.

When one is in alignment with one's Dharma one knows it, for nothing else matters. No matter what the external circumstances are the inner happiness does not alter. The awareness that all is perfect in the Plan permeates everything, every aspect of consciousness. It is all that is. Doubt and fear simply fall away for there is no space for them in this knowing. The rhythms of the universe take their natural course. It is towards this knowing we must strive.

I felt the wisdom and love in these words, I felt the support of the Great Spirit, and felt as though I was coming to know the Joy of soul.

My thoughts were moving from self concern to a more universal understanding. The wings of spirit were gaining strength.

Connection is being made everywhere and many, as I am, are taking flight, feeling not only the wings but the strength beneath the feet, when the spirit descends into matter and the heart is opened.

Explanation of words

* chai - Indian tea

* Vashist - a small village near Manali Himachel Pradesh

* nebuliser - medical aid for asthma

* Higher Self - the part of oneself that is aligned to the voice of soul

* Archangel Michael - a mighty being, spiritual protector bringing forth the Will of God

* Lord Maitreya - the Lord of Love, the Christ Principle, the eastern name for Christ

* Ananda Tara Shan - formerly Lady Shan Tara

* Active Intelligence - the energy of the Holy Spirit manifesting spirit in form

* shaktipat - the transference of the Christ Light through the guru

* dharma - the path of destiny

* aspirant - one who aspires to walk the Path

* disciple - one who walks the Path

.

Deva Wings Publications

Deva Wings Publications was formed on Right Human Relations Day in 1994. Its purpose and objectives are:

1. to spread the Light by creating literature and other materials that help us to understand Spirit and make the teachings of Theosophy (Divine Wisdom) comprehensible to all.

2. to educate people in the theosophical principles.

3. to educate people in spiritual psychology so that we may come to understand ourselves and become that which we truly are.

Deva is a Sanskrit word meaning shining one or angel. The concept is such that the Light and teachings of Spirit will spread over the Earth on the devas' wings.

PUBLICATIONS

www.devawings.com

www.ingramcontent.com/pod-product-compliance
Lightning Source LLC
LaVergne TN
LVHW091257080426
835510LV00007B/302